DIALOGUES ON REALITY

BY ROBERT POWELL:

Zen and Reality
Crisis in Consciousness
The Free Mind
J. Krishnamurti—The Man and His Teaching
Return to Meaningfulness
The Great Awakening
The Blissful Life
Why Does God Allow Suffering?
The Wisdom of Sri Nisargadatta Maharaj
The Ultimate Medicine (Editor)
The Nectar of Immortality (Editor)
The Experience of Nothingness (Editor)

DIALOGUES ON REALITY

An Exploration into the Nature of Our Ultimate Identity

Meetings in California
(verbatim report)

with
Robert Powell, Ph.D.

BLUE DOVE PRESS
SAN DIEGO, CALIFORNIA • 1996

Also available from Blue Dove Press edited by Robert Powell, by Sri Nisargadatta Maharaj:

The Ultimate Medicine
The Nectar of Immortality
The Experience of Nothingness

Blue Dove Press publishes books by and about sages and saints of all religions as well as other inspiring works. Catalog sent free upon request. Write to:

BLUE DOVE PRESS
Post Office Box 261611
San Diego, CA 92196
Phone: (619) 271-0490

FIRST EDITION

Cover and text design: Brian Moucka, Poppy Graphics, Santa Barbara, California

Original cover art by Rob Jacobs

ISBN: 1-884997-16-3

Library of Congress Cataloging in Publication data:
Powell, Robert, 1918-
        Dialogues on Reality : an exploration into the
    nature of our ultimate identity : meetings in Cali-
    fornia (verbatim report) / with Robert Powell, -- 1st
    American ed.
        p.   cm.
    ISBN 1-884997-16-3 (pbk.)
    1. Spiritual life.   2. Reality.   3. Mind and body. I.
Title.
BL624.P67   1996
291.2--dc20   96-24875
                                            CIP

ROBERT POWELL was born in Amsterdam in 1918. After obtaining his doctorate in chemistry from London University, he pursued a career first as an industrial chemist and later as a science writer and editor, in Britain and the United States. In 1968 and 1969, he published nine chemical engineering monographs in use by academic and industrial libraries throughout the world.

Robert Powell's personal exploration of spirituality began in the 1960's, and his quest for self-discovery led him to study Zen and a number of spiritual masters including J. Krishnamurti and Ramana Maharshi. His own spiritual awakening coincided with his discovery of the teachings of Sri Nisargadatta Maharaj. He is the editor of a Nisargadatta trilogy, also published by Blue Dove Press, and the author of a number of books on what he describes as "human consciousness transformation." Powell lives a busy life with his wife Gina in La Jolla, California.

ACKNOWLEDGEMENT

I want to thank Alan, George, Gertrud, Gina, John, Leonard, Mike, Mukesh, Paul, Peter, Phyllis, Ramesh, Sarah, Virginia, and all the others—too many to mention here—who took part in these discussions. Without their valuable contributions this book would not have come about. It is to them in the first place that this work is dedicated, and of course to all serious seekers everywhere.

CONTENTS

DIALOGUES ON REALITY

1.

THE "I"-PRINCIPLE UNDERLIES ALL THREE STATES OF CONSCIOUSNESS

ROBERT POWELL: Welcome friends. I would like to make a few things quite clear. First, in these meetings we are all as it were beginners. There is not the division of the advanced and the not-advanced, the person who teaches and the one who learns. I would like to see this group functioning as a dynamic unit, in which each of us can thrash out a problem and arrive at new insights without being taught by others; that is, one discovers for oneself in a natural, almost spontaneous way how things are. And I would hope that no one in particular dominates these meetings, because there is a danger in that. If one person holds the floor for any length of time, it might be thought that he knows more than the others and therefore has some kind of authority; and that would be incorrect. Because the way I see it, only a beginner's mind can attain some fresh insight. An advanced mind, in the usual sense of the word, means a mind full of knowledge. Now, knowledge of the world is useful and necessary in the world, but to go beyond the world knowledge has no use whatsoever. It is a pure hindrance; to find out about our self, one must have a mind empty of ideas, with no prejudices whatsoever, a mind that can say to itself, I don't know but am open to learning. And in order to learn, it is terribly important to know how to unlearn, to see that our minds are full of concepts, beliefs, and ideologies, that one has made all kinds of assumptions from an early age. Our minds have been acting like a sponge, always absorbing external influences, which is our conditioning. Thus, what we are is pure conditioning. And that conditioned entity thinks it knows something, has some knowledge upon which it can build. But in doing so, it is building upon the wrong foundation, because knowledge is always fragmentary, limited. It is always of thought, of the intellect, the mind, and what we are interested in is not new theories, new concepts, all resulting from mentation, but to go beyond the mind.

Now what I propose to do today is to examine the writings of an Indian sage by the name of Sri Krishna Menon, or, as known by his spiritual name, Sri Atmananda. For those of you who have never heard of this man, the following is a bit of personal background information. Menon, of humble origin, was a householder throughout his life; as a matter of fact, he was a policeman who eventually became a lawyer. His approach was that of reasoned observation and reflection, and he shunned all extremes. Truth, he maintained, is to be pursued neither through asceticism nor through excessive indulgence; it cannot be reached by any method which strengthens the bondage with body and mind. His influence was far-reaching, both in India and abroad, no doubt helped by the fact that he spoke fluent English. He never fulfilled the role of a full-time guru, and his writings are not very voluminous. They include two short books of aphorisms, *Atma-Darshan* and *Atma-Nirvriti*; those aphorisms state the highest truth as he found it within himself. He does not give opinions or theories, but states the simple facts as they emerged from his exploration. And that is what each of us is to do if spirituality is pursued in the right vein: to find the truth, always going from fact to fact, and never, under any circumstances, being swayed by what others say, by mere opinion. In other words, we are pursuing it purely in the spirit of a true scientist, who is not satisfied with anything but that which he has verified for himself. To this end, one eradicates from one's mind all subjective elements, all beliefs, all hearsay statements. Sri Atmananda, to my mind, is a perfect example of such a "spiritual scientist," ever proceeding in a logical, orderly fashion, who can fully substantiate his every pronouncement. So please, let me reiterate before going on to discuss this short essay, let us look at it all together. Don't wait for any particular person here to give you the answer to the problem, if you do encounter a problem.

May I now call upon somebody to volunteer and start the ball rolling in reading a short piece, entitled "I," from *Atma-Nirvriti*. It is the English rendition of one of three articles in the Malayalam language which Menon published in different periodicals at different times. In this very lucid piece he aims at elucidating the true significance of the word "I." He points out that when using this term we may mean a variety of things. Normally, we take it as a body-derived entity, as when I say I do this or that, or I possess such and such a thing. In all cases, I could never make such a statement if it were not for the presence of a particular body. Thus, when "I" is the focus of the activity, it is because there has been identification with a body and an integration of the activities of body, mind and senses. All that is of course within the field of the observed, the known, and so there must be, outside of and separate from that field, an observer, a cognizer, through which we become aware of the body-originated activity. This cognizer-awareness Menon calls the "I-principle" and is more in the nature of a pure witness; essentially he sees this as some kind of superimposition.

He then continues to examine the three states of being—the waking, dream and deep sleep states. In the waking and dream states there has been identification with respectively a waking body and a dream body, which are distinctly different bodies, since the body of our waking state does not exist in our dream, and the body we perceive in our dream does not exist in the waking state. In the deep-sleep state there is a total absence of the mind as it operates in the waking and dream states. Yet, I am present as a changeless entity in all three states, otherwise I would not have a true self and there would be no question of "identity." This signifies that what I call "I" is something totally divorced from body or mind, since both appear and disappear in different states; that is, what I am in reality cannot possibly have any identity derived from either body or mind. If it were otherwise, I might well be schizophrenic in my fundamental nature: each night when I go to sleep, I would be a different "me" than during my waking day existence!

The real self or Menon's "I-principle" is the *Parabrahman*, the Absolute, or Consciousness, in the terminology of Sri Nisargadatta Maharaj. This Consciousness transcends the three states of being and is timeless and spaceless. It is the ultimate Source and Knower of all that is, and exists eternally whether there is a world or not. It underlies all my experiences in the waking and dream states but is itself free from any attachment to these experiences. That is to say, it is absolute since it has no referents, it does not depend. It is its own matrix! To understand this thoroughly is the only condition to get established in the "I"-principle.

Now, did you grasp what he is trying to get at? Did you note the precise and coolly objective approach of the man?

VISITOR: How does he divorce consciousness from the whole? It seems to me he is falling into the same trap of the beginning stages of Christianity in postulating "good" and "evil." Instead of looking at it as oneness, and therefore a facet of the whole...I am also having a little trouble with your beginning statement, in particular with the word "truth." Whose? What is it?

RP: If it is truth, it does not belong to you or to me, it is nobody's private property; so "whose" does not apply...and we are talking of truth as an authentically experienced "certainty"—like knowing that you exist, or seeing that table over there—which is qualitatively different from a belief, an opinion or a theory that in most cases is externally derived and so part of one's conditioning and subject to confirmation or denial.

V: A person's "acculturation" is really his bondage. When somebody says, "I think," what it actually means is "I accept." Those are words, just like "reality." There again, whose? What is it the by-product of? Of what acculturation? And that is why I am having trouble with what Krishna Menon is talking about. He is to me someone who is really saying "I assume," and that is really all we are talking about— not his truth, but his assumptions.

RP: To him, they are truth though; to us they may be assumptions because we have not seen what he sees. For ourselves, it is mere concept.

V: But what I am saying is that as soon as he says "truth," it is written in granite, and what you and I would call the truth is merely an assumption.

RP: I am reminded of a similar interchange between Nisargadatta Maharaj and one of his visitors, where Maharaj said something to the effect that "you take your imagining for facts and my facts for imagination." Ultimately, it is not possible to persuade another through purely rational means. In final instance, truth can only be properly intuited; it can never be conveyed through intellectual arguments. You see, we are dealing here with words; and the difficulty is that anyone who is trying to hint at something greater than the little truth, the relative truth, will have this problem. The words act like a screen, reducing the absolute to the relative, the truth to something considerably less.

V: Without a question. But to me it looks like he is trying to rise above the pain of his own acculturation, to escape from what he is, the true reality of the here-and-now.

RP: That true reality can never be conveyed through any symbols, it cannot be written down whether on paper or in granite. But it can be experienced or realized in consciousness.

Anyone else would like to contribute to this discussion?

V: I did not get the impression that Krishna Menon was trying to separate consciousness from all these other facts, as in the first comment made by this gentleman here. All these things happen to appear in consciousness; you remember he did not say it was apart from it. He maintains the dream appears in me, in the dream-consciousness. The waking state is these ideas as they appear to me. The "I"-principle is steady throughout all this—through deep sleep and all that. So rather than segregating it, I think what he was trying to do is giving us his experiential view that everything really is a whole, as you seem to put it, there isn't a division. We are just looking at it from a different angle.

Second Visitor: Yes, that is quite possible. Part of it, it seems to me, is that he divided reality into different states and I do not believe you can do so. I believe that it has a continuity that certainly consciously or unconsciously has an effect farther down the line or in the next second of time. I don't see how you can say any experience is put right here and gets encapsulated...

V: Do you mean between the waking state and sleep? I think that what he meant is ordinary sleep. You know we have dreams and things like that. In that sense you are distinguishing between these two states. He is saying that the "I"-principle was there throughout, even when you don't have a dream, such as in deep sleep. So he was not separating but for the purpose of description he was trying to show that that was the one absolute feature.

Second Visitor: Could you define that word coinage of "I" for me?

V: I would not attempt to.

RP: He is getting there in the end, but first of all these are the facts, empirical facts if you like, that we have a waking state, a sleep state and a dream state. Right, do you accept that? If not, we cannot proceed. If you do not accept this premise, which seems to me a fact of everyday experience...; we must go step by step into this material. Otherwise, if we don't go together into this, if one or more of us cannot accept that...please voice your views and we will see where we differ. But I think it is a common fact of experience that, as a rough classification, there are these three states. And then, having accepted that, we can proceed and see whether those three states are actually final states in themselves, having no commonality, or whether there is more to it—and perhaps another factor is at work which is common to all these three states. Now here I would like to submit to you: If there were no commonality factor, what would give you the idea that the three states are happening to *you*?

V: Where is all this leading to?

RP: We will come to it. I don't know where I am going. I am just going step by step into establishing the facts of our observations.

V: Are we doing a chronology, or is there somewhere that we want to go?

RP: If you say, I want to go somewhere, you have not got a beginner's mind. You are acting already from an end-point, a goal. And this is what we have warned against...

V: But are you not the sum total of your experiences in life?

RP: Let us continue what we were doing.

V: When you say someone is a beginner, that is to say someone has existed in a vacuum, and in this vacuum they have got nothing; they have become a vacuum themselves. They have been encapsulated in that vacuum and floated down the river of time and never left their capsule. I don't believe anyone is a beginner. I believe that even in the womb there is some questioning, some urge for survival, and that is a sense of shrewdness.

RP: Yes, that may be so but it is on the level of the world, the most basic, material or biological level. In the spiritual area that we are investigating there is only one thing that matters: to have an empty mind; that is the meaning of being a true beginner. The alternative is to be prejudiced, in however subtle a form.

V: There is such a thing as curiosity and there is such a thing as "written in granite." I think when someone accepts a series of word coinages, remarks or whatever the case may be, while he is open to say "I accept this and will walk," then I don't think it is a prejudice. What I think it is, it is merely an acceptance of something that you know as against something that is unknown to you but with an openness to change it.

Second Visitor: Can I say something?

RP: Go ahead.

V: The way I understand Krishna Menon's argument is that a question is raised. All I heard was a question. If I think, feel, laugh, do physical things, do mental things, slave, what is behind it? I hear this as a question: "What is this 'I' behind all these different things I do?" All I heard was that question, no answer.

SECOND VISITOR: Did you hear that at a given moment the "I" can be any one of those?

V: It is actually behind it.

RP: The difficulty arises when we bring in our knowledge, and our thoughts start wondering about these various points. Whereas without all that knowledge and those opinions, we can see immediately the point Menon is trying to bring out. And I think what this gentleman said earlier is another form of expressing this difficulty: we have the desire to know what it is all going to lead to. We may have some idea in our minds of what the self is and we are approximating what we see to that idea or ideal. But if you know nothing about it, then you are like a scientist in the laboratory carrying out an experiment and not knowing where it is all leading to. And I want to approach it in that spirit.

V: In other words, you find it preferable to determine where we are at the moment.

RP: Yes, indeed, without looking beyond, I choose to deal with the here-and-now.

V: Nobody is going to carry on with the position taken in Menon's treatise, but we just heard it and wonder what he means by it and keep an open mind.

RP: O.K., shall we go on? Shall we further examine whether we can consider his statements for fact or whether, as our friend here said, the man is deviating from fact and making assumptions. Now that is terribly important to find out. If your statement is right, that he is making a dissociation, then I would throw away his booklet.

V: Well, I don't think there is a right or wrong, there is only a viewpoint.

RP: No, this is our normal worldly way of looking at things within the field of our conditioning. We are not concerned with viewpoints or opinions whatsoever, because viewpoints are always fragmentary ways of seeing and limitations of the truth.

V: There again, you seem to have found what the truth is. I have not been that fortunate.

RP: I may not have been either. But I am just pointing out that if what we call truth is really that—the totality of all that exists—it cannot be a fragmentary or partial thing. It would be incomplete and just as there is no limit to the number of points of view, so one would need an infinite period of time to attain it. In other words, it would be unattainable. So my approach to this problem is totally different from yours. As stated from the outset, I have voided myself of all opinions, all knowledge, and having emptied the mind in such a way, I can call myself a total beginner. But for this, I watch myself. I watch my own mind accepting mere relative things as absolutes, being sensitized towards likes and dislikes, in short being conditioned—so that none of this may take root. Rather than attaining the summation of an endless number of fragments—the partial views—I enter the state before any point of view, any definite molding of the mind, has yet developed, which equals the state before my birth. I see this as the only effective way of dealing with my conditioning which has been going on ever since I was born and to which I had never given permission. All else clearly is only manipulation within the field of conditioning. When you finally wake up to it, and you find out for yourself, from your own experience, that there is a totally different way of functioning—call it spiritual life or whatever, it does not really matter—then you are on your guard. And this then becomes a discipline, not in the sense of the Zen people, or all the other religious people who say do this or don't do that, but a discipline in the original sense of the term, a "learning," because you will always go from fact to fact, and you will no longer be pressured by opinions or viewpoints. Mere opinions don't count. Your opinion is as good as the other person's opinion, or vice versa. On that level we will get nowhere. You know, Vedanta means "the end of knowledge," and our current concern is what lies beyond the knowledge which is ever confined within a subject-object relationship.

But we have not finished yet with Krishna Menon in getting the most out of his essay. By quibbling over some minor points—issues that lie on the very fringe—we have missed the main thrust of his argument, which may be the real liberating factor. The three states that he examines—the waking state, dream state and deep sleep state—are obviously interconnected by that "you." For one thing, there is a certain overlap between the states, for example the waking state and the dream state "spill over" into each other, as when the dream continues to "haunt" us in the waking state, and when the dream is obviously based on our waking experience. And the deep sleep state is connected with the waking state, because the oblivion it provides is a mere interval in the waking state and does not wipe out all my memories and cognitive functions. So the cement that binds together the three states, their underlying unitive factor, Krishna Menon calls the "I"-principle. And because the three states are ever-changing, in a flux, they cannot be my true identity. The states themselves cannot have any identity, being mere appearances in manifestation. Therefore, what am "I"? My real identity can only be their underlying cause, which is unchanged through waking, sleeping, dreaming—that is, the "I"-principle; and therefore in my real self I am apart from and unaffected by the three states and the travails associated with them. I am beyond space and time, I am the Cause before all causes. Therefore, I am all that exists, has ever existed and will ever exist.

V: Ah, I am beginning to see! Something has suddenly clicked. You have resolved for me the problem of the truth being individual and incommunicable. It is clear to me that all formulations by anyone as mere word coinages are part of the relative state Krishna Menon talks about, and that all these relative statements of truth, which can never be universalized and thereby validated for all, are not the Ultimate but are mere thought structures. I understand that the entire range of conceptual views springs from the Ultimate, which is the truly universal although inexpressible, and that being in that very state, through transcendence of the three relative states, is living in Reality. And because the "I"-principle transcends the so-called "individual," we already live in and are part of that Reality. It is now seen not as an enormous claim that smacks of arrogance, but is a fact for all of us, although apparently most people are not yet aware of this Truth. Thank you very much.

2.

A Maverick Who Makes Some Valid Points

OBERT POWELL: I am happy to see so many old faces here today. What I have decided to do for this meeting is to ask Alan to read a passage from a most unusual book that he has discovered, *The Mystique of Enlightenment* by a namesake of J. Krishnamurti, a man called U. G. Krishnamurti—not because it is indispensable for our spiritual guidance or anything like that, but because it is interesting, stimulating, and it might, perhaps in some unintended way, be very instructive as well. There are many pitfalls if you take this work too seriously, which you will realize as we go into our discussion of it.

Visitor: [Reading pp. 55 and 56 from the quoted work]:

> What is keeping you from being in your natural state? You are constantly moving away from yourself. You want to be happy, either permanently or at least for this moment. You are dissatisfied with your every-day experiences, and so you want some new ones. You want to perfect yourself, to change yourself. You are reaching out, trying to be something other than what you are. It is this that is taking you away from yourself.
>
> Society has put before you the ideal of a "perfect

13

man." No matter in which culture you were born, you have scriptural doctrines and traditions handed down to you to tell you how to behave. You have commandments to obey, virtues to cultivate. You are told that through due practice you can even eventually come into the state attained by the sages, saints and saviours of mankind. And so you try to control your behavior, to control your thoughts, to be something unnatural.

We are all living in a "thought sphere." Your thoughts are not your own; they belong to everybody. There are only thoughts, but you create a counter thought, the thinker, with which you read every thought. Your effort to control life has created a secondary movement of thought within you, which you call the "I." This movement of thought within yourself is parallel to the movement of life, but isolated from it; it can never touch life. You are a living creature, yet you lead your entire life within the realm of this isolated, parallel movement of thought. You cut yourself off from life—that is something very unnatural.

The natural state is not a "thoughtless state"— that is one of the greatest hoaxes perpetrated for thousands of years on poor, helpless Hindus. You will never be without thought until the body is a corpse, a very dead corpse. Being able to think is necessary to survive. But in this state thought stops choking you; it falls into its natural rhythm. There is no longer a "you" who reads the thoughts and thinks that they are "his."

Have you ever looked at that parallel movement of thought? The books on English grammar will tell you that "I" is a first person singular pronoun, subjective case; but that is not what you want to know. Can you look at that thing you call "I"? It is very elusive. Look at it now, feel it, touch it, and tell me. How do you look at it? And what is the thing that is looking at what you call "I"? This is the crux of the whole problem: the one that is looking at what you call "I" *is* the "I." It is creating an illusory division of itself into subject and object, and through this division it is continuing. This is the divisive nature that is operating in you, in your consciousness. Continuity of its existence is all that interests it. As long as you want to understand that "you" or to change that "you" into something spiritual, into something holy, beautiful or marvelous, that "you" will continue. If you do not want to do anything about it, it is not there, it's gone.

How do you understand this? I have for all practical purposes made a statement: "What you are looking at is not different from the one who is looking." What do you do with a statement like this? What instrument do you have at your disposal for understanding a meaningless, illogical, irrational statement? You begin to think. Through thinking, you cannot understand a thing. You are translating what I am saying, in terms of the knowledge you already have, just as you translate everything else, because you want to get something out of it. When you stop doing that, what is there is what I am describing. The absence of what you are doing—trying to understand, or trying to change yourself—*is* the state of being that I am describing.

RP: Now who is going to comment on this—this fine piece of prose?

V: I would be curious to know about the author.

RP: Why?

V: Just curious.

RP: [*To Alan*]: You are somewhat familiar with the author. Maybe, you would like to give us a brief sketch of him, because a lot of it is not generally known.

Alan: It is hard to know how he became what he is. Even he himself says he is not quite sure about what or how it happened...Probably it would be most interesting to understand where he is really coming from. He was very deeply involved in all the Indian traditions, and with many, many gurus of various kinds, from the Theosophical Society onwards, through J. Krishnamurti, and many places, many other teachers. Years of effort and struggle lay behind him before he came to this, the "natural state of being" that he talks about, where he constantly emphasizes the fact that no amount of effort, of thinking, will bring you to it, because the very instrument you are using for reaching that is the greatest obstacle to it and perpetuates itself through its actions. That is the gist of it.

Second Visitor: According to J. Krishnamurti, the thought creates the thinker, and at the same time the thinker is the thought; so then it is as though thought creates itself. There seems to be a logical contradiction somewhere.

RP: But if as you say, the thought creates itself—for the thought does not really think itself into being, but appears spontaneously, isn't there also some supreme logic at work? How could it be otherwise?

V: But what is the "I" really? Is there any permanency there?
It is kind of scary that thinking is always there until you actually die.

Second Visitor: U. G. Krishnamurti said that thinking would continue until you are a corpse—that is still not contradictory.

If we take thinking as where our self is, it really is a big problem. But if we see thinking simply as just another mechanical function and that its content is not really personal—because all thinking, all thought, comes from all of us, at the same time—then there is no issue. There really is no problem until you identify with thought and say, that's "me," or you feel that you are the thought or hold the thought.

Third Visitor: The thought is the "I" as well as the seeker. Going back to what this lady says, it seems there is already a division because I am what I am seeking.

V: In my own experience I find there are moments when we are not thinking, but they are so…"momently"…they go through and then we are back to thinking again, at least for me.

Second Visitor: I don't know, because as soon as you say there is a moment I was not thinking…it seems a very slippery statement.

Third Visitor: I only know through experience, and there is no way that one can describe that moment.

V: But is it an "experience"? I don't know what word would describe it.

Second Visitor: There isn't a word for it.

V: If there is no thinking, then you are silent.

Second Visitor: No, but if there is a moment of silence, the mind grabs it and puts words around it, and that's the end of it.

RP: Very nicely put.

V: That is very true.

Second Visitor: J. Krishnamurti calls it the observer and the observed, and tell us that they are one. I find what you have read sounds just like J.K.

RP: It *sounds* just like J.K., parts of it, but the essence of U.G.'s teaching, if you can call it that—because he denies there is a teaching—the essence of his book, is that no matter what you do, you are not going to break out of this limited state of consciousness, simply because this alleged "transformation" is a biological phenomenon; it is not a psychological happening at all. It is recorded in the coded messages we carry in our genes that determine what we are and what we will be. He goes as far as saying to the people around him: You are wasting your time, go away—don't bother me. Of course, that's an obvious gimmick, because why does he talk in the first place?

Now consistent with his reasoning is that there should among those coded messages also be one that determines your breakthrough out of this limited consciousness into this state of—if I say "enlightenment," he won't accept it, so let us say "changed being." And either you've got it or apparently you haven't got it. So if you haven't got it, tough luck!

V: But how did he come to this conclusion, though?

RP: He does not explain that. To him that is a fact; it is not a theory to him.

V: You are either born with that, or...

Second Visitor: But he also says that it can happen to anybody, and he (U.G.) is not special. There is no distinction; it is just as much available to anyone as it is to him.

RP: If you happen to be lucky enough. He says so. If per-chance...by luck...it happens...but then it is determined by one's genes. I don't determine my genes chart. So whatever he may say to anyone, if he is serious about it, this genetic explanation, then it is not available to most people.

V: No, it is not very fair! [*laughter*]

RP: Also, he says that it is primarily a physical change. There are all sorts of physiological phenomena that take place, and his body underwent certain fundamental changes. For exam-ple, he lost his masculinity, and became androgynous...
     Have you any further comments on this?

V: No, except the more you explore the man this way, the more contradictions you will find. The only reason I read that particular chapter is that the point he is making there could be very valuable to all of us.
     As you say, it is similar to J.K., but it is like listening to it from a different angle. There really does not seem anything spurious in what he said in that particular chapter. It is applicable to us, because my mind, "me," is always in move-ment, always seeking something, and I know it is that very movement which keeps me away from my natural state of being—or simply being, without any search, any demand. As long as my mental attitude is such that I identify with that thought, the idea that there is something special to be achieved, then I have to be like a dog chasing its own tail. I think that's very frightening.

RP: I think the main point is that if he is right about his the-ory, then everything is futile, obviously. If it is all a matter of either/or, either you are born this way, that is what it amounts to, or you are not born this way...he says it is a mat-ter of only one in billions who can break through. And if that is so, then we are just wasting time and many other people, many spiritual seekers, have been wasting their time, too—because it is purely a physical, biological event. Now if you accept that, then that is the end of all such activity. Personally, I don't accept it, but you will have to find out for yourselves.

V: What about awareness, is not that part of it?...that could be increased?

RP: He says "choiceless awareness" is a gimmick invented by J. Krishnamurti and is "phoney baloney," as he calls it.

The other important part of the book, I think, is—and you have to see where he is misleading us—when he is talking about the negative approach. We in this group have talked about this on many occasions. Now he says the negative approach does not really exist: you have made it into a positive approach. That is his broad generalization in the matter.

As you all know, we have ever been very careful to state that we will approach matters entirely in the sense of looking at what we are here and now, not from the point of view of some idealized existence which may or may not be a reality. We will look at our way of functioning which is so obviously unsatisfactory, because we are in conflict, in sorrow; we are always striving to reach out to something that we do not even know...we have done so out of a deep inner dissatisfaction throughout our lives. And this is one of the reasons why we are searching for something which we call "spiritual." Most of us who are interested in spiritual things have a basic dissatisfaction with the everyday life, as presently lived. Because if you are totally satisfied, you don't need all this; then you live with that state of superficial contentment until it ends or the body drops. Now we have been saying in these meetings: Let's look at the way we function at the moment. Let us forget about the way we might be able to function; in other words, forget about all these goals, because that's what all these conventional religious groups are doing. They have an image of what man could or should be.

V: The "Golden Rules"!

RP: Yes, that is his behavior. But we are going into it even more fundamentally than that. Man should be "perfect," whatever that means. He should be in the image of God. And when you have a goal, an ideal, you are all the time approximating yourself to that ideal, and therefore you are in the clutches of time—because it is always tomorrow that one will attain. And while you are striving to attain that miraculous state, you are still there with all your misery and conflict. So obviously, it is getting you more and more into a mire of self-deception, thinking that you are arriving somewhere, making progress and in actual fact you are just the same as you were yesterday.

So we have been saying: Look at the false, the way that we operate currently, which is full of falseness. Because we pursue all these limited ideals, we don't even know what we want. We want "happiness," which is a mere word, and we always try this way and that way. We are striving to find fulfilment because we feel incomplete within ourselves. So we pursue fulfilment through wealth, through sex, through possessions, through all kinds of activities—and yet it always eludes us. Isn't that right? We may have a momentary satisfaction; but it never lasts and we are back in the old state of dissatisfaction. So that is what we have been saying: Look at all this, before going on to some highfalutin ideal or goal. Because once you have that goal, you have rules, a path, with guidelines like all the conventional religious teachers have given us: Do this and don't do that. And then you are no longer an authentic human being, because you are just repeating what somebody has told you...something that you don't know anything about...you are merely following.

Now the difference between U.G., where he attacks and

demolishes the negative approach, and what we have been saying and discussing here among ourselves is the following. He is saying you have made that negative approach into a positive approach, because you are deluding yourselves, because through that negative approach you are still trying to get something. So it is just a subtle way of kidding oneself, of a method, a "how-to."

On the other hand, what we have been saying here is to forget about *all* goals; in fact, we have been emphasizing this very same point, excessively so almost. We have been saying there are no do's and don'ts...there are no guidelines. You must totally forget any other state that might be attainable. Just look at and concentrate on what is here and now. Once you do that, which is following a hundred percent negative approach, you immediately begin to discover how you function and create misery for yourself. Upon seeing that clearly, something else falls into place all by itself. *You* don't do it; this whole process that is continually taking place within us is in thought. Thought is always striving to reach some delightful state. It wants gratification to itself. All the time, trying to attain, it is in conflict. So when you look at things with or through thought—and that is where the crux of the matter lies, a point which U.G. emphasizes very much—you will ever be defeated, because thought will translate what it sees according to its own conditioning. In other words, you will not look with clear eyes, you cannot, because thought creates the thinker, the ego, the "I." And the "I" will not allow itself to be demolished. The definition of the "I" is that it is a dynamic entity that is always looking out for its own security, trying to expand and aggrandize itself, so that it has greater security. Once you have created that entity, the "I," it is the end, you are finished because you are totally in its clutches.

So to look at one's thought process requires a very special way of looking. It needs looking without a background—that is, the entire thought mechanism, which is always saying: this is good, that is bad, always deceiving itself, must be inactivated. And that is what J. Krishnamurti refers to as "to look without the observer." When the observer and the observed are one, then that is an entirely different kind of seeing. That is a seeing in which you are not really involved at all. It is as our friend here observed a little while ago, in that split moment when thought is resting and the mind has somewhat subsided, that you can see clearly and only then. But as long as thought is active, feverishly as it normally is, to give sustenance to the ego, there is no possibility of seeing one's conditioning. Do you see that?

The observer is the sum-total of the conditioning, and that is the entity that looks at conditioning! So obviously, the observer has a vested interest in what he observes and will seek to protect it. Therefore, such a process will never under any circumstances lead to a fundamental change. It cannot, and thought will always try to find some satisfaction and will even abuse what we are pointing to, this spiritual state, or call it whatever you like—liberation, enlightenment—it will even downgrade that into another kind of ordinary gratification.

We ever want something. Have you ever been in a state that you don't want something? Only when thought is quiescent, only when your mind isn't there. As long as your mind is there, you are searching for something, always "on the make," in a subtle sort of way.

V: I don't agree with that!

RP: You don't agree with that. Have you observed yourself?

V: I think a person can control his thinking.

RP: What is it that controls the thinking?

V: Well, your own mind.

RP: Well, there you are! Because the mind and the thinking are not different—the continuous flow of thought is what we call the "mind"—control is not possible. Control would only be possible if it concerned two completely separate and independent entities. But that is here plainly not the case. Ramana Maharshi said in this connection, it is like the policeman trying to catch the thief who is himself. The policeman is no different from the thief. You see, this is a very good example of how we are deceiving ourselves. I am not being personal, madam, I am talking in general. Of course, what you are expressing is so universally valid: we think we have some kind of super-truth within ourselves that can control all this falseness, a higher self that can manage the lower self. The point is that this "I," this ego, has innumerable mechanisms at its disposal for deceiving itself. The resulting conclusion, or the action flowing from that conclusion, is always the end product of the interplay of all our thoughts and concepts. So on the level of thought, it is not possible to rise above our own ego-sphere.

You just have to give up on the mind altogether if you understand what the mind is: a bag full of tricks. Don't just take my word for it; each of us has to see this for himself and come to that point where you have totally exposed the mind and can't be deceived any longer.

So when you have come to that point and see the total impossibility of achieving a breakthrough in and through the mind, then you are in that state that U.G. has described, where you just back off completely; you are totally helpless. When you are in that condition, and you see that by yourself and through yourself you cannot do anything at all, only then can something be triggered off. But don't try to quieten the mind in order to get something; this is an obvious device that thought will seize upon when it hears something like what we have been saying just now. It will try another trick upon itself: it will hypnotize itself that it is quiet, concentrate on a mantra so that it will fall asleep. But the mind that has fallen asleep is not a still mind. A still mind is a mind that has seen through all this, realized the futility of its striving. It can't go any further; it has tried everything to no avail. And in that moment of giving up, of letting go, there is a break in its usual activity. Then the mind falls totally silent, which is a blessing.

This moment may not last very long. So the mind comes back; the mind has just had a wonderful experience. It has been free of burden for a split second or a little longer. So what happens? It says to itself: I must get this experience back. It was marvellous, I must have it again. And the very fact of trying to regain it means it will not happen!

V: But as long as it is getting "experience," it is still the mind that is at it.

RP: Yes, but that moment of silence we talked about is really an absence of experience. As one of you said earlier, we have not even got a word for it in our language, so we call it an "experience" of silence for lack of a better term.

V: But Robert, don't you think that was the one interesting thing U.G. brought out in this thing, the condition of what he called the "parallel thought process" going on. We don't take it that way. I take it that I am seeing my thought, or I have an idea and I can preserve it as such and he is very clear when he says that what actually takes place is the mind splitting itself up into parallel movements of thought, so while one thought is going on, another thought is moving alongside it, judging it, and these images reverberate from one to the other. So I tend to think, like I believe most of us do, according to what you've said, I am standing at a distance from the rest of the crazy thoughts and I can kind of control them. What he is trying to expose—with such deep insight—and it is very difficult even to understand it, because most of us don't realize there is this parallel movement of thought...

Second Visitor: Because that movement is always there?

V: Yes, but do you see why it is so strong, so powerful? Because in the essence of the parallel movement of thought lies the image of myself as a concrete entity. I really believe that is "me," that is my ego, which is judging whether or not you are clever, whether or not I am clever, or something like that; whether my thought is moving in the right direction. It is constantly censoring everything and pretending the process to be different from all the other thoughts inside of me; it sort of gets separated out from the rest of the thought process, but it is just the same thought process.

Second Visitor: That is which makes it difficult to see, because we see from that "I."

V: More than that. It may be that which is responsible for the whole thought process itself, because it seems to be the center of gravity like the sun around which all other thoughts spin and are kept in motion. Because of the clinging to that image of myself as an independent "I" who is clever enough to eventually get out of this whole quandary that we are discussing; therefore all thought is dependent upon that, all thought circumnavigates it. And I keep calling it "I," because I have split up things into the observer and the observed, or, if you like, the thinker and the thought, but they are both pure thought, purely mechanical movements.

Second Visitor: So the one keeps the other going; they are not separate at all, they are together.

V: You are right, you have caught the point. But then what can you do in such a situation?

RP: And the odd thing is that without this inner tension within thought, the very thought momentum would collapse;

the mind would not be there at all.

In my book *Crisis in Consciousness*, I referred to a mechanism which, I think, is similar or identical to U.G.'s parallel movement of thought. I was describing an ongoing adjustment of one's behavior by means of a psychological feedback system, which is kept alive mainly by the "second-thoughts" we have—the afterthoughts which sneak in and aim at modifying the thoughts that have passed in an effort at "self-correcting." Remaining largely on a lower level of consciousness, these thoughts are not dealt with adequately in the here-and-now, and so leave a psychological residue. Thus, they add to the karmic reservoir that determines the destiny of the body-mind entity.

Hubert Benoit, in his book *The Supreme Doctrine*, talks about an "inner lawsuit" which is continually being enacted in our subconscious mind. I believe he is referring to the very same mechanism that we have been discussing. These are all valid descriptions of aspects of what goes into the process of "becoming," which is really what sustains the "mind."

V: Does that come from the subconscious, that parallel function you are talking about?

Second Visitor: I wonder about that, the subconscious; it is always going on, I am identified with it and I think of the subconscious of being way back in the brain cells and memory, and influencing me from some distance, but this is right here, all the time. If you look at me, insult me or say something that may give me a funny idea about myself, then that springs into action, instantly; it goads all my activities, it is my notion of myself. So it is right there. I don't have to go to a therapist and dig at it. It is always there, as much as the consciousness is there.

RP: It also depends on how much you repress the observation or the thought. If the truth that you are observing is sufficiently unsavoury to you, you will repress it and it goes into the subconscious. However, that is a purely artificial dividing line, separating the subconscious and the conscious. But this idea of the parallel thought, as U.G. calls it, has actually been institutionalized in Indian religion, where they talk about the higher self and the lower self. The higher self is the self, which we think is the noble part; and the lower self is that which we do not really like, is not very respectable. So, they have institutionalized that split and they can hide behind it...

V: You don't believe in the "superconscious"?

RP: All these are words, madam. These are artificial divisions.

V: I know, but then give me your definition of "mind."

RP: I don't give definitions of mind. The mind is beyond definition, because definitions are only on the level of thought. Any such definition could never be more than a kind of circular argument, for like can never determine like.

Once you really *look* at thought, you are beyond thought. Obviously, your definitions then are no good anymore. You can give a definition on the level of science, of what our physiological mechanism is like, or what a brain cell is, you can give definitions in that realm, but you can't give definitions that concern our most fundamental being and functioning. That would be absolutely futile, because it means to be caught within a set of words.

Words are merely symbols, abstractions; but this goes far beyond words. You have to understand it for yourself, you have to see it in action. Then you won't ask for definitions any longer, once you have seen clearly what we are doing to ourselves; how this artificial entity, which we call the "I" or the ego, has come about and how *we* create it from thought, because thought itself is totally fluid, void of any entities. We have formed this static entity, the ego, from this fluidity. So merely see the unreality of that entity. Then, where is the need for definitions? That's the beauty of it. This is not science that we are doing, not spiritual science. There is no such thing! You can't put this into a set of equations.

V: Sir, you speak of fluidity. I want to inquire into a question that arises from this reading, this notion of the biological program, *when* one is to be enlightened, because to me this brings up a very deep question, of looking at it as a biological or mechanical sequence of events. Then, what he calls "enlightenment" is a consequence of a certain mechanical process, just like a clock. The alarm goes off and that is when it happens. And the difference between the word "consequence," the mechanical result, and something which originally happens...I find I have to look more deeply into the word "happens" and what we mean by something happening, and related to that also the words "hapless" and "happy." Does it not imply some kind of freedom or fluidity or space wherein there is, albeit it may be choiceless, a possibility of Creation; there is not just a mechanical, linear process.

RP: Well, I can't answer for U.G. I don't know how he has worked it out; he just makes this blunt statement that...—but maybe the key word to this problem is what he says about...he does not want to call it "enlightenment," as a matter of fact, he calls it a "calamity" because when these physical changes took place he was in great pain for several days—this change is acausal; that is, it has no cause. Now I don't know if you can reconcile his theory of genetic origination with acausality.

V: It does not connect.

RP: How can you? I don't think there is a way.

V: It sounds like what he is talking about is "mutation." It is something that just happens.

Second Visitor: It is a problem, for how do you find the right word for something that does not fit into categories?

RP: The other part of his conclusion, which states that consciousness transformation is acausal, I wouldn't knock at this stage. He may well be right there; all the great *advaitic* thinkers have testified similarly. The subject is so vast that it would warrant a whole discussion session by itself.

My more serious objection to his theory is this. Fundamentally, the body and mind are one. We have split these two. In actual fact, what we are is a psychosomatic entity, a piece of "psychosomatic machinery" if you like, and to single out the soma, as he does, and to give that primordial importance, does not make any sense to me. What he is saying in effect is that the body cells are more important than the consciousness. Whether you understand yourself or not does not count or is secondary. All that is overridden by the condition, the structure, of one's cell material. So, with one stroke of the pen he has set back the clock to the era of the materialist philosophers, who believe that matter is the basis of all reality. And at the same time, it reinforces our erroneous notion that we *are* our body, for how we function depends exclusively on our body cells. So by saying that man's ultimate transformation is primarily biological, physiological—physical, if you like—then the basic reality, the primordial reality, to him, is the physical world, doesn't that follow logically?

Now my point is—and I have driven it home on many occasions in my books and so on—that what we call the physical world is not a primordial reality, because without consciousness we would not even know, there wouldn't even be, a physical world. There is consciousness first; otherwise, you couldn't talk about the body. What do you mean by "body"? Body is merely a set of sense impressions, coordinated, interpreted by the brain, emerging into this consciousness. That sum-total of these impressions we call "body." So consciousness is prior to everything—a primordial reality. Everything else comes subsequently, arises within consciousness and eventually sets again within that consciousness. Thus, this whole world is within consciousness. It is not like they used to believe, the scientists of the mechanistic era, that the body produces this consciousness. Do you remember that, not so long ago? There are still scientists who believe that. The very latest physics indicates, however, that this sharp demarcation between matter and mind is no longer tenable.

V: Regarding consciousness, isn't it so that some of us are conditioned to think that consciousness is a function of the ego, whereas one can also look at it differently and say that ego is a malfunction of consciousness?

RP: But there is something, a different consciousness that is not limited by the ego. There is that limited consciousness; and there is a consciousness or Awareness which is timeless and spaceless, since it is not based on memory—the changeless matrix which itself is the source of the changeful and without which you would not even be able to designate anything as changeful. But do you agree with me, can you see, that consciousness is more basic than the soma; that the soma is a product of that consciousness?

V: Yes.

RP: So, what becomes of his argument then—U.G.'s argument that this process is a biological one, primarily? It doesn't make sense, does it? Also, one wonders why he keeps on talking, because what good does it do...to tell people that they're out of luck? That's really all it amounts to. It's just for the chosen few.

V: Well, maybe he's a prankster.

RP: He may be. I feel that is so, I feel that very much. When I first read this book, which was lent to me by Alan, I said to him, "I feel this book was written tongue-in-cheek, to a large extent, if not all of it." And he has the background of a prankster, too. We needn't go into that here, but it's known.

3.

MORE ON
THE *VIA NEGATIVA*

isitor: I want to know how to "look" without my mind, because I think we are doing the opposite all the time.

Robert Powell: There's no "how" of course; you just look, you just have to *look...*

V: That's scary...

Second Visitor: Is it really scary, or is that just an idea we have about it? I am not asking you to answer because we've got a lot of fancies about this sort of thing. We really think that it's scary because it's already projected and what you see may not be favourable to one's image, and all that...a lot of things are already pre-set-up, and I really wonder if there is anything to be frightened of...I'm just asking this question...everything we do, we approach it from a point of view already...and that's part of the problem we have...to be able to look without bringing in our views, all these various things; the mind does not function like that...it has no trace of simplicity...and the very essence of mentation, at least the way it seems to me, is movement...it doesn't like to just look, just see...and stay with that.

V: I think the fear is, maybe you're guilty, or you're hiding something from yourself.

Second Visitor: But isn't that a mental projection, again?

RP: But all that's still a partial looking; if you look partially then you have all these ideations come in. On the other hand, if you look totally, without that background of thought, there is no further thought entering, there's no judgment. You just perceive everything the way you look at a mountain on a clear day...I mean, you look at it as it is, purely and simply, not as you think it ought to be. You don't fantasize, you don't say that mountain should be greener or it should be less barren, you just view it as it is. And so, in the same way, you look at yourself, as you are.

V: When I look at myself, so to speak, then I have these feelings of fear and what not, because then I'm focussing on myself. But isn't looking also seeing the reactions of other people and listening to the sounds of...?

RP: Yeah, sure. Everything, it isn't restricted. When we say look at yourself, it means yourself in relationship...because without the relationship, there's no self. There's just an emptiness. The self, or what we take our self to be, comes into being through the relationship, through the thought. Let us not get lost in verbal descriptions, really. This is where it matters to do it, to see how we are a network of thought, how we are full of relationships and ideations.

V: Which is what U.G. Krishnamurti says, that thoughts are not my own. All of us here have thoughts, but none is *my* thought...

Second Visitor: Also, there is thinking of fear. This is very important, because both of you said it differently. Did you notice? She said she was afraid to see herself as she is; you said that even while I'm seeing myself I feel fear of what I might be seeing or what I am seeing...and I wonder if it really isn't more true the way she is putting it...if you really are seeing, there is no sense of fear, it's just seeing, it's a different kind of thing. But if I am looking at thought from an observer point of view—an observer who has an opinion, whether what I am looking at is good or bad, if that's called looking, then it's just another idea—it's an idea looking at an idea. Then the whole thing is a mere trick. So I have to really see if I'm actually looking, and not just thinking about looking. This difference you can only see very clearly as you're looking. You will know just then if you're just thinking or actually seeing when that parallel movement is there or when it is not.

V: I agree with the lady when she says it's scary...it is scary and yet it's exciting too and perhaps we can go so far as to say that the mind is fear, and going out beyond the bounds of the mind is like becoming an outlaw, and it's also getting toward where the energy is...it reminds me of some people who never leave their houses...

RP: Agoraphobia...

V: For ten, twenty or thirty years they've never been outside their home...and to me it's like that, going outside the mind, actually going out, to really look, to see. It's like being naked...facing the fear and yet that's where the energy, the excitement is, being an outlaw, going outside your mind.

RP: I wonder if the fear doesn't come in because we are not willing to face up to our real nature. When we start looking this way, one sees one is totally nothing, one has no self-importance whatsoever, and the mind resists that. I think that fear is because you are in a state of *partial* looking, you're looking with your mind—the mind, the ego, which doesn't want to see itself destroyed...it's still fighting, always fighting for its life.

V: That's what perpetuates this "parallel thinking."

RP: Right. It's division...it's a trick by that center. It has split itself up into the respectable part and the part you can kick around. So the very fact of this division of the higher and the lower self is nothing but another trick, another way for that center to manifest itself. And therefore that kind of looking is like going around in a circle, it will only perpetuate the problem.

V: It's still, or supposed to be, the "observer." It is still "me" looking from my point view. It is also important to talk about what she meant by "exciting." Yes, I know that kind of feeling. And that's a common experience and is also a form of the observer. The other looking is so neutral, it's like seeing in a mirror...the mirror does not get emotional as we do about everything, which are pure reactions of the observer.

Looking is simply looking...something that most people have no concept of any longer. Sometimes, when we were very little, as an infant...I have a baby of around four years...there was a period when it was very clear she was just looking, pure and simple, no axe to grind, no dividing...no liking or disliking...pure awareness. That kind of awareness, to see what I actually am, is a whole new experience for us. And it involves neither terror nor pleasure nor excitement, nor anything negative at all...it's simply looking. The only thing that feels the other things is the ego which is pretending to look; but it's not a true looking...

Second Visitor: But to me the excitement is part of the process...the experience of looking is an ecstasy in itself...it is an ultimate kind of energy or liberation...there is a power there...there is not only excitement, but it is also ecstasy or "ecstasis"; there is freedom.

V: The mind is trying to sort of describe the indescribable...it is indeed indescribable...the nearest you come to it, I think, is an energy, you have a tremendous feeling of energy. But it goes beyond anything mental, it's a different kind of thing. Otherwise, we are discussing experience, an ecstatic experience, a happening or something...when it happens to me then it becomes part of my conditioning. This is a very complicated problem. I know what you're saying, it's very tricky to put into words, but it does involve something very powerful.

Second Visitor: I think you can form an attachment to that ecstasy, that enlightenment, and then you're hooked on the kick of insight, until you just relax and stop trying to *be* or to *get*, and realize that the happiness was from the very beginning and it always is, and there is no "getting." Getting is only the getting-in-the-way of it.

RP: The getting satisfaction will only stop when the "receiver" has come to an end—the receiver of that satisfaction. As long as that's there, which is the "you," no matter what you do, you will be going around in circles.

V: This has always helped me, to realize that everything I think of is a concept, and I have to get rid of every concept I've ever picked up from the day I was born and whatever I brought with me. And that involves the world of opposites; I have to get past those opposites. Even looking at a mountain, the moment we look we judge it, it's either pretty or ugly, high or low, or something. But if we can forget opposites, especially "good"...it's easier to forget the "ugly" maybe and think it's O.K. to think of something "good," but we have to look beyond that too, because good infers bad.

That realization to me is a big help.

RP: Especially in human relations, and not so much when we look at nature. I think nature has an overpowering sense...when you look at a river or a mountain, you are not likely to moralize about it. But when you look at human values, immediately your moralistic background with which you've been educated springs into being and you say, this is good, that's bad...this is a bad guy, that's a good guy...you don't look at him as a process that is part of the world process or the totality, but you look at him as a fixed entity that has a label attached to it, many labels, and most of these labels are moralistic. You like and dislike. All your likes and dislikes come into being from that background, always within the pairs of opposites, as you say.

V: But why do you want to get rid of opposites?

Second Visitor: They are the results of my concepts.

RP: They're unreal—products of the process of division, which is the mind.

V: I want to get behind my concepts, what really *is*.

RP: It's not a matter of getting rid of them either...it's seeing them for what they are: worthless, ultimately.

V: Opposites are concepts, also.

RP: Invented by the mind, like high and low. Where is high, where is low? Purely arbitrary—relativities.

V: To me the answer isn't so much getting rid of them but to rename them...normally, what we do with opposites is we shift from one to the other, we go away from bad and want

the good. We don't like confusion, we want to be enlightened, and so on. The one thing the mind doesn't ever like to
do—and this could be the only thing that might make a real
difference—is simply to remain with what you are. You are a
world of opposites, you are that. I am that. I watch it. I'm
interested in that. This is actually what I am, like a mirror
reflecting exactly what's happening. So instead of being
Krishnamurti or some other great philosopher, I just stay
with where I am: purely looking, and I'm not jumping from
one opposite to another. But if it happens, if the opposites
switch, that's exactly where it is.

Second Visitor: That's where it is, at the moment.

RP: But you see, there is more to it than that, with respect to
the opposites. A process of comparison lies at the bottom of
it. We always compare what we are today with what we were
yesterday, we want to better ourselves, and we look at this in
time; and we also compare ourselves in space…with others
who we think are better, more fortunate, and we are envious
of them, we want to approach their level, whatever they've
got in the way of possessions or attributes. So to me, this
everlasting comparing is the essential play of the opposites.

V: [*The gentleman is from India*] This comparison is totally
cultural. I see that in the Western cultures it is much more
important than for example the culture I was brought up in.
And even the language symbols that we use. . . the word for
this ego, the "I"; in the English language it is capitalized, and
this word that you use for the obvious instrument of seeing,
is pronounced the same way as you pronounce the word for
yourself. So it's just a totally different emphasis on this individual entity.

RP: But aren't we totally the product of this cultural conditioning? Is there anything authentic in us? Look at all your

thought. All of it is derived from the culture.

V: Wouldn't you say the problem of the observer and the observed—the "me" keeping distance from the parallel thought movement, so to say—is identical everywhere; however, the shape of it varies tremendously from country to country. But the ego problem is identical. The things they talk about in the *Upanishads* are the same problems that we have every moment of our lives; it is all there.

RP: It may be that the values have different attractions; perhaps in the West we're more interested in material things like wealth, good health and outward appearance. But then you might say in the east they are still caught in this comparative process, too, and no less so, but possibly in an opposite direction. If you are a beggar, have nothing...go about devoting all your time to spiritual endeavours, maybe then you're high on the totem pole there.

V: Your attachment is to the spiritual.

RP: You are a *sannyasin*, as they call it, you own nothing. But if you were in the West, you would be "nothing," on the ladder of social values. In the East, having nothing, no material possessions, and being a *sadhu* or a holy man, you are very high on the totem pole. So again, it's culturally conditioned, but the particular values differ from country to country. However, the process is the same. You had a question, madam...?

V: You chose the negative approach, and I wonder why you chose that...?

RP: The positive approach is just what we have been talking about; always wanting to get something, and then you are caught, because you call it spiritual but in actual fact you don't know what "spiritual" means. So to you, it's still a worldly thing.

V: In other words, when you say the negative approach, you mean to negate what *is*, is that correct?

RP: To see the false as the false, and to accept what *is* and not what *should be*. It is positive in one sense, namely that you accept a hundred percent what *is*. I mean, you accept it: it is a fact.

V: Yet, you call it "negative"?

RP: I call it that because I negate any projected state, which all religions are postulating...call it nirvana, heaven, liberation, or *moksha* as they do in India...I don't care what exactly you call it. To negate that completely, and to look at what *is*, right here and now.

V: The positive approaches of other teachings and religions are all concerned with trying to become something else, something higher. And they have various methods to attain that. This is all traditionally part of the positive approach. You might be able to get a clearer idea of this if you just think of it as the image of a photographic negative. All the film does is take in the impression, it refuses nothing, it is not concerned with wanting to change anything, with being different. It's just simply like the negative of a film or a mirror which is receiving the impression of what actually is. And that's not something we are used to...the mind only works in a positive way.

That's what this chap (U.G. Krishnamurti) makes such an issue of...that no matter what the mind does, it's still the positive approach. Anything at all we try to do with our mind, whatever trick or whatever word we call it, will again be the positive movement of the mind, our conditioned past, trying it this way, that way, more subtle, less subtle, but still it will tend to be the positive approach. I think one has to see this very, very clearly.

So anything I do or not do about my present condition will probably again be another form of the positive approach. And no matter how many times we try to talk about or explain it, it's hard to realize. The mind is very cunning about this. It's more like a policeman trying to catch the thief who is himself. This is very, very peculiar. If that's the case, I have to say to myself, well, what can be done then? It is a tremendous dilemma. I have to stay with this. This could be a key for us, to stay with this a little longer.

RP: And what J. Krishnamurti talks about as "choiceless awareness," and he also particularly emphasizes this, can be abused by certain people who misunderstand him. It is a negative approach, totally negative, choiceless awareness. It is staying with what is there. But if they are just words to you, and you haven't really understood what Krishnamurti was talking about, and you use it as another "how-to," another method to get something—enlightenment or liberation or whatever—you can abuse this and use it as a trick, but then you have tricked yourself.

I remember a lady in the Buddhist Society in London many years ago who was a marvelous example of this. She was a devout Buddhist, but was also somewhat interested in the teachings of Krishnamurti, of which she had a smattering of knowledge. She had picked up this phrase "choiceless awareness," and had read about it a little bit and thought she was applying it in her own life. Here was a lady who had many psychological problems. And one day she told me that it was marvelous how this teaching of J.K. had helped her and was making her more aware of herself, as she put it, and how she was therefore using this choiceless awareness whenever she felt a psychological disturbance. Any time that she was experiencing conflict, she "used" this choiceless awareness, and hey presto!—after she'd done it, the pain had disappeared!

She was so happy about it, but I didn't argue with her, I didn't go into it with her. I just thought she will have to find out for herself, sooner or later. What she was doing, she was utilizing, twisting this choiceless awareness...only doing it in a lopsided manner. She was being...maybe, to give her the benefit of the doubt...she was choicelessly aware, but only during those episodes in her life when there was mental turmoil, whenever she had psychological problems. She did no such thing when there was pleasure, when everything went well...to hell with choiceless awareness. She didn't need it then.

To her it was an obvious means to an end, and so a positive approach under our definition of the term. And I think this is a brilliant example of how even the most supreme truth, whoever has expounded it, may be exploited, may be corrupted by a person who is desperate to continue finding new, exciting experiences, trying to find a way of dealing with sorrow, and not understanding it. He will just pick on something, from any teaching that pleases him. It's a selective approach, do you follow? That person doesn't take the teaching as a whole, but just takes a little bit of it to suit himself, and then thinks that he's got it. This is only an example but also a warning to all of us how slippery this whole field is. Because we are so likely to pick up a fragment of a teaching when it appeals to the mind and so make it our own, but we don't really understand what we are doing. We take it out of context, and then it has become a positive approach.

V: Can that be harmful?

RP: It is just that it will lead nowhere. It will be a continuation of the old process of the mind, always grinding on endlessly. And, on top of that, like in the example I gave, one is deceiving oneself.

V: But she has relieved the pain. . .

RP: You see, that is a temporary thing. And because she is doing that, she is setting herself up for a greater fall. Because if you are given to pleasure and don't understand the pleasure-pain principle operating in nature...for there is such a law of nature—it's a fact—that when you pursue pleasure you court pain...pain will come in its wake, as surely as night follows day. When you live in such lopsided manner that you push away all kinds of pain, try to eliminate it, remove it from your life, rather than understand it, and you just live for pleasure, you split yourself in two—it can't work, it won't work. Because pleasure and pain are not separate, they are one movement and constitute another pair of opposites. Now by cutting it in half, you are courting great danger. There will be tremendous psychological implications if you do that and are not facing the reality of what you are.

V: It's possible that she had to go through something like that. That might be part of the mind process.

RP: But most people never get out of that, because it strengthens the illusory process.

V: It does not go down to the bottom line.

RP: There is no deliverance in that.

V: To ask about this negative approach, perhaps we have difficulty with what "negative" means to us, because...

RP: I've just explained it, in this context. It should be clear.

V: Well, may I then elaborate on that for a moment? Because what you said about the photographic negative struck me, and I thought in the next moment, I guess an empty cup is negative, and negative in one way of looking at it is "receptive"...but to us, because of our conditioning, it may be difficult, because "negative" means saying no, it means a counter-positive rather than negative-receptive kind of thing.

RP: Well, it all depends on the context. I've explained what I mean by "negative." I think I can't explain it anymore clearly than I have already done, and this is generally accepted...the *via negativa* it is called. I don't know whether you've heard that term. It's a well-know expression in the spiritual literature. It is total negation of projection from the mind. And at the same time, total acceptance of what *is*, living with what *is*. That's what we mean by "negative."

V: But there may not ultimately be any real difference between what Robert is saying is total negation and choiceless awareness.

RP: Those are the same. Exactly, there's no difference.

V: So we should not be too confused by the description of that lady and maybe ourselves, because we may have done this earlier ourselves in using choiceless awareness as she did. For her it was almost like a therapeutic thing, like you take a yogic exercise or something like that. The chief question, however, is: Is it even possible ever for us to *use* choiceless awareness...or is every form of using it just a continuation of a mental image and projection of something higher, and therefore by definition impossible to be true choiceless awareness when I am choosing to do that. So we may not really understand what it means, this complete, total negativity or what choiceless awareness is. Isn't it rather something closer to what you were talking about before, when the mind is not seizing...when it is not wishing or wanting or projecting in any sense at all, but you simply are seeing...just in being still, with not a movement at all.

There are tremendous implications as to what choiceless awareness is and what it isn't.

Every time we try to use any of these things as a technique, we are back into the positive approach. So it is a very subtle thing, and the only way you ultimately can see any difference and meaning in this, is actually in the seeing itself. For there will come a moment when the mind takes over and seizes it, and then it's choice again...

V: I have a new feeling for "negative." It's negative-receptive, non-projecting.

Second Visitor: Of course, the Christian Bible has a good word for it —"non-resistance."

RP: Yes, you might say that. And also, "Judge not," talking from the Bible. It's the same thing, judge not. That sums it all up. No opinions, no judgments, no set values, just staying with what *is*.

V: It's very subtle. Because even what he said just now, this thing of being receptive, it's a very clear way of looking at it but dangerous. The reason is this: I think that's the right way to be, O.K.? It really does sound correct. If I'm just receptive to *you*, then I'm receptive to *myself*. So I've taken this position; it does become that way, and it seems right and so I do it. This "I'm doing" is already a movement away from this total negativity. It's so subtle...

Second Visitor: Another tool!

RP: Yes, it has to be passive, totally passive—no "doing" of any kind involved! I think an alternative term that Krishnamurti used in the earlier days was *passive* awareness—which is easy to confuse, also.

V: It's so easy to confuse all these terms.

RP: You see, words will not get us anywhere. You can come close to something, close to a feeling, giving the person the feeling for what it is, but beyond that, you can't go...and one must have an intuitive perception of some of these insights. They can't be *given* to another. And then also, as Alan said, I'm not even sure whether this lady who said she was using choiceless awareness when dealing with her suffering, I'm not sure whether it was really that...

V: She believed it...

RP:...or whether she was just using those words. She believed it maybe, but whether it actually was...I'm not sure. It may not have had anything to do with choiceless awareness.

This is the crux of the matter, what Alan said. I think it's very useful to stay with this for a little while and look at it, because if you don't get it, this is *the* stumbling block, the greatest hindrance. Otherwise you can never go beyond.

V:...the pain, in order to be relieved from the pain, you should go into it, become the pain and feel it...be the pain, and live it through...

RP: *Be* the pain, right, right...but not just the pain.

V: For that's choosing. Krishnamurti does not say...be aware of your painful thoughts, he says, of *all* your thoughts, not just selectively. Pain is just one of your feelings. It could be anything else.

Second Visitor: Not to focus on the pain, something that you want to get rid of...

RP: Right. It's a subtle difference, but a fundamental one, because it defeats the whole spirit of it. Because then it is a means to an end, to be free from something that bothers you. In other words, it's another way of gratification, getting rid of some particular conflict. Why not *look* at the conflict? *Be* the conflict. Look at everything. You should look at the disturbance and find out what's going on, how one functions. But when the primary reason is to get rid of it for the sake of getting rid, then it is a kind of gratification—that's the way I see it.

V: He says that of beauty as well. To go into beauty, if you are aware of beauty, you're going to be part of it.

RP: Everything.

V: Now that's conscious awareness as well.

RP: Could we say this...go one step further now...that the mind cannot initiate choiceless awareness?

V: I would think it needed to.

RP: It cannot. Because there is an inherent contradiction. The mind is by definition a center of choosing.

V: The mind cannot initiate anything....

Second Visitor: It does, it chooses.

RP: But it cannot go beyond itself, in other words. Whatever it does, is a projection of itself, by itself.

V: In music, you have the same expression for the awareness of beauty...to be choiceless and not compare with anything that happened before...because if we experience ecstasy through this, then there's a yearning for a repetition of this ecstasy.

RP: That's what we were saying.

V: And yet we need to be ready for this experience of beauty and this oneness with beauty, whatever it might be.

RP: But if you make that the primary goal in your life, to repeat those experiences, you're back to the hunt for gratification, you're not concerned with the truth of things.

V: But he [*that is*, *J.K.*] talks about being so conscious that one's life should be lived as though one were living with a rattlesnake in the same room...that is, you are ready for whatever experiences are presented to you.

RP: But the mind cannot be ready for it. As long as the mind is preparing itself, it won't happen. Because the mind is the stumbling block, the mind is the hindrance, the *only* hindrance...

V: You have to have some posture in life though, for one's being right where one is and we begin from there.

RP: That's what choiceless awareness is, that's where we begin from. But then the mind...

V: And the experience could occur at any time, whether it is here or...

RP: Any time.

V: But that isn't choosing, isn't thinking.

RP: But why prepare yourself for it, madam? If it comes it comes, if it does not come, it doesn't and that's alright, too. As long as there is thought, and whatever is in thought, it will block you.

V: I don't see that...

RP: If there is an anticipation, or if there is a yearning, we are off the *via negativa*. Only when the mind is absolutely still, and there is no anticipation whatsoever, are you on track, so to speak. As long as you are looking forward to an "experience," the mind is in the saddle, the ego is in command, and nothing new can occur. Thought has tremendous powers of projection, you can visualize all sorts of things, but it won't be the real.

4.

WHAT
AM I REALLY?

Robert Powell: Today I would like to discuss the question of what knowledge, if any, needs to be acquired for our spiritual emancipation. Maybe, in this connection, there is nothing wrong with not-knowing and it isn't a matter of "knowing" at all. Because, as we have seen, the old consciousness is based on knowledge, on knowing what to do, on rules for living. But in actual life this is not going to help us at all, as any situation in life is ever new, and if you approach it with the old, with knowledge, with a blueprint, then you will miss: Your response to the challenge in the moment will be totally inadequate. I think most of us have experienced that; we go to great lengths in preparing for certain important meetings, or events, and unless we are dealing with technical matters, such preparation always falls flat. It does not actually help you.

We saw in our previous meeting that the mind knows only this kind of procedure; it will re-act from the past, because whenever it is faced with something in the moment, in the now, in rush all these memories, all these experiences. And whether one likes it or not, it is a purely mechanical process; we may think we are in control, but that is entirely illusory. Thus, there is no fresh response, no appropriate action; it is always the memories and the past experiences

51

that dictate the action, which is therefore not really an action at all but a re-action. And so we carry this tremendous burden of memory, the thousands of yesterdays, which one thinks is needed for one's psychological survival. Upon waking up to all this or it being pointed out to us, we look at the state of affairs and say to ourselves, "I mustn't, I must try to get rid of all these memories."

So, how does one get rid of these memories? Now as soon as you put it in those terms, you have created a new problem, because the question is basically meaningless. You cannot get rid of these memories by any action whatsoever; and in fact the very consciousness that asks the question is the cause of the problem.

Then what is one to do? When I am faced with something that is a mere re-action from the past and wish to deal with it through the application of conscious effort, I am fooling myself to think that I have changed anything, because what results is again a mere modification of the old consciousness that continues with the same tricks...I feel this is terribly important for all of us to see, that we are constantly deceiving ourselves when talking about a new man, a new consciousness or a new age of awareness, when in actual fact, nothing at all has changed. We carry on with the old way of life, merely giving it fancy names. And the real difficulty in discussing this type of issue is that we approach everything from the standpoint of the old consciousness.

For example, you may have had a glimpse into a new way of living, and I, on the other hand, am firmly wedded to the old way, the way of the intellect, its actions and re-actions, and its concept-building processes. You have had an experience in the Now, which you are trying to tell me about as adequately as you can. And I, for my part, approach it with all that mental baggage that I carry, my many experiences, my entire background. And never the twain shall meet, because yours has been an actual revelation, a vivid insight; and I hear your words but immediately correlate them with theories and statements from various authorities. And so there is no real contact, no real communication between us. This is one of our problems.

When one attends a meeting only once and has never really gone into oneself, it is virtually impossible to get anything out of it. One meeting is just not enough. The reason for this is that if you tackle one issue, and want to understand it fully, in all its ramifications, this requires that a lot of related issues be grasped as well. For instance, somebody has just entered here fresh from the street, and hears our talk on the necessity of observing oneself in the moment. Now most people will take this to mean "introspection." Isn't that right? But introspection is exactly this process of re-action that we have been talking about, the seeing from the background, from within thought. And that has nothing to do whatsoever with self-observation, which is pure observation, in which there is no censor, no evaluator. So when one talks about observation, this needs immediate clarification; the different ways of observing need to be gone into. Merely to state, "Observe yourself," will fall flat, because people will take it the wrong way; and generally they will pursue the well-worn thought tracks. After all, can anything else be expected from a conditioned mind?

So the moment you tackle one issue you immediately get involved with another, related or underlying issue, and that in turn leads to further issues. It is almost like a chain reaction. And none of these things, in my view, can be tackled really lucidly, thoroughly, without coping with the most crucial issue of them all, which is finding out what I am, who I am, what is the "I"? If I delve merely into various secondary issues, I will remain for ever sidetracked. I will always be on the surface until I have explored the main issue of man's identity, What am I?

For some of you who have gone into this matter, and have arrived at the profound insight that there is no such thing as an individual entity, everything lightens up and you are beginning to see things in a different light; they start making sense. But if, on the other hand, you have never given these matters any attention, a breakthrough in one's understanding will remain almost impossible to achieve. And that insight, as we said before, cannot be given to you—it is your job to get it. It is my job to get it. Everyone of us has to acquire it for himself. There are no authorities.

So a meeting like this should be a mutual exploration in which we discuss things on a basis of equality. Maybe you are learning from what I am saying, when I am relating my insights to you—I am not ramming any theories or concepts down your throats—but at the same time it is a two-way traffic: you are relating your insights, you tell me how you see things and I am listening and learning, because as you are telling me of this deep insight you have had, I say to myself My word!, I have never looked at it in that light! Here apparently is something entirely new, and if I don't understand it right away, I don't say to you: Oh yes, it sounds interesting but I can't see it this way, I disagree. Because that would be absolutely meaningless, to agree or disagree. Either one sees it or one does not. As you are telling me of the profound discovery you have made and are trying to put into words, I am perhaps not ready for it yet. But somehow the words get stuck in my mind, and perhaps one day while walking along the beach something you told me suddenly makes perfect sense, and I now clearly see it for myself. This, by the way, is how things work out in practice; it has been my actual experience.

We have gone into these matters many times, yet we have to keep in mind that each of us has to do this for himself, and that to look at an issue in isolation is almost impossible; life is to be viewed holistically. Unfortunately, most of us look at things fragmentarily. The way we currently function, each of us is a fragment. We are not total human beings, because we are calling ourselves an American, a Russian, a capitalist, a socialist, a Catholic, a Muslim, a Jew, and so on; we are calling ourselves so many things, and by the mere fact of attaching a particular label to what we think we are, we have cut ourselves off from others with different labels. Isn't that true? In this way, we have cut up the whole into fragments. Then, from the point of view of the fragment, we try to understand that which knows no fragmentation whatsoever. So we ourselves are the cause of the fragmentation: We do it with our labels, with our opinions, with our beliefs, our experiences, we are the ones who have created this totally divided world.

As I said, it is necessary to see things holistically; otherwise, you will never get to the bottom of anything; it will be an abstraction, a partial view, an intellectual thing, and never a total insight. But here lies the difficulty: You can only see things holistically if you, as the observer, are no longer a fragment, for a fragment will always see things along the lines of its own fragmentation; but in order to deal successfully with this fragmentation, you have to be able to see things holistically. So we have a perfect double bind situation!

Why do we come upon a double bind situation every time we try to attack a fundamental problem? The reason for this, in my view, is that the very formulation of any problem as a mental construct or concept—i.e., in dualistic terms—is a form of abstraction in which something essential gets lost; also, it necessarily entails a basic contradiction. It is like solving a mathematical equation in which our basic parameters are indeterminate or fuzzy: the answer will come out as ambiguous and therefore not meaningful. In other words, another example of "garbage in, garbage out"!

Now to go beyond this double bind situation is only possible if you understand the process of fragmentation on all levels. At this point, automatically, immediately, we come to the question: How did this fragmentation come about in the first place? That is logical, is it not? If fragmentation is such a big problem in our understanding of the world, then we should give attention to that first of all. And in order to understand how fragmentation has come about, one must understand this whole mechanism of thought, because that is where it originates. Also, if one does not understand what one is, and one has erroneous ideas about one's identity, then fragmentation is inevitable. Since we have this body and are totally identified with it, the mind adopts a mold of thinking in which it is a person, an individual. And that is the beginning, the germ, of the fragmentation process.

So it is absolutely essential to go into the whole process of thought and the way we identify ourselves with memory, with images, since that is where everything starts.

Visitor: I honestly don't know if people understand fragmentation.

RP: But they see that the world is fragmented; they see the political parties and the religions and all that.

V: But I wonder if anybody actually sees that the moment there is thinking, in that second, instantly everything is being divided and subdivided, broken up into pieces, and identified and defined, as different from each other. In other words, the whole is here all the time; everything exists but the moment I begin to think, do I see that the whole process of thinking is itself a movement of division? It is always dividing, all the time. And when I divide, I am presenting myself at the same moment with a different sort of universe. Each of us is doing it in a slightly different way. And that is really what thinking is. But most of the time, is it not true, we look upon thinking as a constructive act, an effort to arrive at a better place. We don't realize that thinking is always a movement in division.

RP: We are totally lost in thought and we never examine the thought process. What you are saying is essentially what I was getting at, that we cannot stand away from thought and look at it objectively and go into its basic mechanism. And unless you do this, you are caught in this thinking, because you are unconscious of the wider picture. You are a victim, as it were. You are no longer in control. If you are pushed hither and thither by the very same thought process, you have no autonomy. Right?

V: But isn't this our consciousness? Is not this what is always working, our thought process?

RP: It always operates; that is our consciousness, unfortunately—the consciousness of division. Only occasionally, the mind falls into a stillness, in which there is that wholeness without the mind having any power to disturb it. The mind is then still, for just a moment, and consequently, thought has quietened.

V: There seems to be a problem here in dealing with the subject, because, as you pointed out, we are approaching it from the point of consciousness which is always divisive as thought.

RP: The problem is made more complex because you can't just kick out thought altogether, you can't say, "All thought is useless," because there is a definite place for thought. You see, we need thought on the worldly level. Thought is a tool, and a useful tool at that, but we extrapolate from it. From its usefulness on the material level, we apply thought on a psychological level, and that is the trap. We are not aware of where thought is applicable and where thought not only has no applicability at all but where it becomes a definite danger, a psychological danger.

V: Can there be thinking without conscious thought?

RP: What do you mean? You mean subconscious thinking?

V: No, without the individual being aware of the thinking taking place.

RP: It is always like that: thinking without the individual being aware. It is only when memory comes in...you currently have a thought, say about how beautiful the weather is. Immediately afterwards, there is a memory of, for example, last week's foul weather, how then you were caught in the middle of a rainstorm. So it's immediately afterwards that the "thinker" or the self-image comes in. But in the moment itself, there is just a movement of thought and feeling—a perception with a thought; the thinker comes in afterwards, not initially. But let it be, the thinker comes in, you can't stop him. However, that is not a problem, not the way I see it. Psychological tension arises only when the thinker enters and makes demands, and says, I must have more of this, or less of this; that is, when he tries to control the experience; the experiencer then becomes all-dominating, all-powerful.

In the ordinary thought process, on the material level, this is not an issue. You have a technical problem and thought works at it and possibly solves it. It is not a question of striving emotionally or becoming highly involved with it. If that happens, you inevitably move from the physical level onto the psychological level, as in the case of a scientist who is working on a problem in his laboratory. As he is operating on the level of the scientific problem, or pure intellect, his mind works very smoothly. But then his thoughts change, he becomes psychologically involved; there takes place a definite shift in his vision, his way of functioning. And he says to himself, now I must succeed, because I want the Nobel Prize. I give you this just as a simple example. His whole thought process gets corrupted at that moment, from applying thought as a tool, the thinker comes in as a psychological entity with all its images, and then the striving starts: "I must...I am involved with that experiment, I must succeed, I must find something new. Because if I don't, my whole career is at stake."

V: And the moment the thinker comes in, the impression

internally is of a fragmented universe. The paradox here is that the thinker never really does come in. It is only an impression, because there is no thinker, never really has been. The thinker is only the movement of thought itself.

RP: The thinker is also another thought, a creation by and within thought. This is part of the process of inquiring into one's identity: To see, that that which we call the thinker is basically another concept, tied up with various images that we have of ourselves, like the scientist in his laboratory who has the concept of being a scientist, being prominent, wanting to become more prominent, to obtain these prizes, gain recognition by his colleagues—all images that stir him up.

V: But is it not an extraordinary thing that it is a mere concept of an entity that gives rise to the impression of a divided universe all the time? Isn't that a strange thing? But the moment that the concept is not there or does not interfere—for example in a child of let us say, one year, or the scientist, who, as Robert said, is actually immersed in clear thought—the divided universe does not play a part. It only occurs when we have this concept of "myself" as a separate entity, different from you, different from the rest of the world. It is a strange sort of mental trick that goes on all the time.

RP: It is very interesting and truly amazing, as Alan puts it, that that concept assumes a life of its own. We live a life of concepts and we are walking concepts, you might say.

V: We identify so much that we have become concepts ourselves.

RP: Until somebody challenges you and asks you the question: Who or what are you? Then you start to find out about these matters. And then you come to the extraordinary realization that you are not what you think you are; you are nothing of the sort, in fact you are Nothing and that is all you are. Presently, you only are what you think you are. As Alan said, it is a thought, but there is no actual thinker. And that is a marvelous, beautiful insight, which is the beginning of an understanding on a holistic level. Until you have that essential insight into what you are, everything else is a struggle to understand and you will miss, you will not succeed.

V: It is almost an essential insight into what you are not. In other words, if you see your self-image as a mere concept, an emptiness, a non-entity, then the next question that has to occur to any reasonable person is: If this thing that I always think I am, this idea of a continuous self caught in time and space and this body, if this really is not what I am, then what am I? Am I anything at all: That is a very special question, I think, and something a person has to go into very deeply. I may be something; I may not be this, this fleeting thought, this notion I have of myself. This probably is not real at all; it keeps changing, it is constantly presenting images; it has no depth to it at all, no palpability, no substance whatsoever. If this is not "me," my true self, then what am I? This is the real question for us. Otherwise, everything is nothing but a game, a pure dream. Why do anything, if that is the case? But if I am real, and have a real self, where is it and what does it consist of? What really is my reality? I don't know whether we have ever got into this question? It is a tremendously critical question, because otherwise if we do dismiss the notional self, the false conceptual self, then what is left really? We have got to come to this and get a feeling of it; if not, the whole exploration is always going to be just a silly game. It does not really have anything to it at all.

RP: If you had really let go of that body identity, Alan, you would not be asking that question and you would know the answer to it immediately. In fact, you would *be* that answer! But you may have to convey the answer through your silence only. How do you expect to give an answer about the eternal and infinite in terms that derive from the finite and fragmentary? On this high level, can you still deal with such questions in the usual philosophical-conceptual way? And who is asking the question anyway? You see, all these issues are interrelated, and if one works through all that and experiences one's real identity, there is absolutely nothing more to be said. For one who has had that extraordinary insight of no longer being any particular identity as normally conceived, but instead being the totality, or the dynamic manifest, all concern about anything, all movement of the mind, all thought on the matter, ceases. There is no longer any urge or need to do anything at all. Nor *can* you do anything, for you are the totality! And the totality being complete in itself, movements in time and space are never for that totality, only for parts within that totality.

So it is just the opposite of what you postulated: exploration takes place and has meaning only up to the point that this explosive insight is reached; thereafter there is not even an entity to do the exploring. The insight we are referring to is the very fulfilment of the exploration.

But while we are still probing and using all available means, including thought, we may want to examine another issue, a very interesting one, the question of freedom which to me is closely connected with what we have been discussing so far. Let us go into that for a little while.

We have various ideas of freedom, but I repeat we have all that knowledge, and knowledge on this level is totally useless, so any ideas of freedom you might have, you must forget. Because, again, they are mere concepts. Please follow this a bit, because this is terribly important. If man is functioning, as we have seen, as this interminable chain of reactions, he is always re-acting from his experience and from his knowledge. And even if he says to himself, as he does—we have had people here at these meetings say that—O.K. I will stop it, I can see that man is re-acting, there is nothing new, I am always a victim, I am always re-acting to whatever is happening to me, I will stop re-acting, I won't react anymore, or I will start doing the exact opposite, the funny thing is that he is still reacting. Can you see that there is no such thing as "stopping reacting"? Because if he merely does the opposite, or abstains from re-acting, it is still a re-action. You may call it a re-action to a re-action, or a negative reaction, but here two negatives don't make a positive! He is just fooling himself if he thinks that he is no longer re-acting. (It is simply the nature of the mind to function in this way; that is why an appropriate appellation for this mind would be the "reactive mind.")

All this is, of course, the question of choice. How does one make a choice? And can man ever be without choice? Is there such a way of functioning? Most of us think that choice is the hallmark of freedom. But the way I see it, it is the hallmark of slavery.

V: Is not choice itself an illusion?

RP: That is what we are trying to say and demonstrate to you. I am pointing to it, coming to it. Choice is always based on thought, on mentation. And even if I say to myself I will not re-act, you cannot do such a thing as not-reacting. So although choice appears to us as an exercise of free will, what is the significance of that impression so long as the "me" that exercises the free will is an unknown quantity? Since the "me" is totally time-bound, any movement, any "choice," by that entity takes place within a deterministic framework, and so one will never be free from the wheel of life.

V: The phenomenal manifesting part that either acts or reacts, is that us anyway? Is that the self?

RP: That is a different question. There is no such thing as an operational self, but can you see that there is a totally mechanistic process going on? Even leaving out the question whether or not there is an entity—obviously if you go into it, you will see there is no entity, there is just this mechanistic process.

V: But if there is no entity there, then the whole issue of free will and determinism, all that sort of thing, has no meaning; it is not even a question.

RP: In conventional terms, the whole issue of free will—this is what you are hinting at, I think—free will versus determinism...

V: I am not thinking of that...whether it acts or does not act...

RP: But I am putting this in the form of an antithesis, because most people who talk about free will, see the alternative as determinism. They see free will as the opposite of determinism—a totally free action as against a totally unfree action. Now I maintain that within that antithesis of free will -determinism, there is no solution. On this level there is no synthesis emerging, the reason being that the underlying assumptions are incorrect. There is no answer from such a formulation.

There is, however, an answer which is totally unexpected, which transcends both free will and determinism, because all that which goes on, this whole chain of actions and reactions, is on the level of thought. And so within thought, there is never freedom. There cannot be. We can have new inventions by thought which it dubs as free and creative expressions, but those are the results of a mechanistic sequence. It is still a time-bound process, based on knowledge, on memory, so to approach it on that level will never give us any relief, any freedom. Real freedom can only come beyond all that, beyond the thought process.

V: Your answer then is to negate all thought.

RP: How do you do that? How do you negate thought? Please go into this, because it is a leading question that you are putting. Can you negate thought, and if that negation is achieved, is it not a re-action to thought again?

V: By saying that I am negating, it is another thought.

RP: Exactly.

V: Who is the negator?

RP: You see how we get caught in the same thing, over and over again.

V: But then...we may never be able to negate or dispense with the thought.

RP: That's another thought! To say, "we may never" is another thought. It is a projection from what we have thought, what we have experienced.

V: So my effort to deal with thought is another thought.

RP: Exactly. And for all that, we are still ensnared in thought! Zen Master Bankei compared such futile efforts at cleansing thought with "washing off blood with blood." See this clearly, because you can't quibble with facts. And it is no good to say, I am going to find another clever way. First, see the fact. See it and stay with the fact, and understand that thought is helpless, is absolutely powerless.

V: It is helpless, but I am trying...

RP: He is still trying! [*laughter*] Like squaring the circle.

V: But beyond thought lies this bliss, this...

RP: Ha...no, no, no. How do you know what is beyond thought? Because somebody writes or talks about it? Suppose I talk to you about there being something beyond thought, it is marvelous, it is blissful...I may be a liar, I may be saying something to create a reaction in you, or I may have a vested interest in saying that. Be so careful, be absolutely reliant only on your own insight. You are the authority, nobody else is!

V: All right, Who am I? If I dropped dead right now, how I am feeling right now, I may be about as happy as I am going to be at this particular instance, or as blissful or as free of thought.

RP: Anything is possible. It is possible that you may die...but in these matters speculation will not get us anywhere, and that is not the point here.

V: So I might as well be satisfied the way I am feeling right now, because I may drop dead in the next second.

RP: You may not. You may have to live for another fifty years, or twenty years or whatever. And to you it may be a punishment or a blessing, that is not the point. We don't know. We are speculating about the future. But we are living in conflict now, by and large. You may have a moment that you feel good. You may feel fine right here and now, because we are talking about matters in general. So for a moment you forget that you may not have a penny in the bank and your wife is about to leave you, or whatever. And for a moment you sit here, and the mind is distracted, as it were.

V: But it is still working.

RP: It is still working, but it is not working in pain. You are not mulling over the same old problems. But they are sure to come back, and what we are concerned with—what one is asking, we are not working towards it—is: Is there a way of living that is totally different? A modality that has a different perspective on life in which there are still problems but the problems have, as it were, their own place and they do not overwhelm the mind.

V: I am very attentive to what is being said and what is here. But that is still another thought and I am the actor.

Second Visitor: Is that a thought? That is a good question.

RP: That is the point where we ended last time. We brought in this question of listening and time, and I think we missed the point when you asked: Attention, isn't that a form of time? Attention surely is timeless. If I am listening, I am all there. Being totally in the present, I am not thinking "about." That may come afterwards. But in the moment of giving attention, listening, I am there, in the present; I am Presence itself. I am not in time; the past plays no part whatsoever in giving attention, in being aware, nor does speculation on the future. If I have even the least expectation (as desire or fear), I am not fully attentive but indulge myself within the realm of thought. I am indeed totally fulfilled in the moment. What prevails is a state of total freedom, and death has lost its sting.

5.

ATTENTION, THOUGHT AND IDENTITY

Visitor: We should realize that attention, the paying of attention, is itself understanding. You don't have to collect new ideas, bring them together. Now that's hard for us to understand, because normally we put different ideas together and try to make a formula of the whole thing...But that is not true.

Robert Powell: It is like listening to music. You listen, and you understand or you don't. You don't have to think, to have ideas or concepts about the music in order to appreciate it.

V: That's an abstraction, music; it is not verbal.

RP: No, but it is in the present. You listen to it; you can make it into an abstraction—that is the difference between a musical score and the music actually being played and listened to, when it is not an abstraction. The abstraction is the menu; the actuality is the eating. But most of us are satisfied with the abstraction, which is really an extraction, a taking away, a distilling. Right? When I distill something, even when saying I retain the essence of something, I have diminished the original and only a small part remains, which is the abstract. It is not the whole but again is a fragmentary thing.

So when I use words as abstracting tools, such as "I" and "you," the result is inevitably another abstraction. When I say "Alan," it is a mere label and not actually Alan him"self"; it is a code word. But in itself, beyond serving as a code, it is only a noise. And in using the word "I" so glibly, without understanding that "I," we erect an entire erroneous world from which a multitude of further erroneous concepts follow. It also represents the original division—the beginning of all division. And then also I say "my thought" and "your thought." We all say that, don't we? But there is no such thing as my thought or your thought; there is only thought. This is a very important point to grasp. There is only thinking. But all of us have this idea: it is my thought, my property. Please go into this. Because as long as you think along those lines, you live in a divided world.

Also, we have this body, and identification with it, and as a result we have a center, a point of reference, a "mind"—that whole collection of memories, images. Then I always talk about my thought, my "this" or my "that." But thinking is just thinking. Essentially it is impersonal, but we have made it into something personal. "My thought," "my opinion," when it is just a thought—even my opinion is essentially only a thought without certificate of ownership attached to it. It has nothing to do with "me," that is the joke of it. Can you see that?

V: Are you saying then that thought is universal?

RP: You might say so. Even that word "universal" does not really get to the heart of the matter. Thought is thought and the personal element is false. Thought is always in a flux, ever changing its color, its content. But it is impersonal. It does not belong to a person. That is all I am saying. I am not trying to impose a mold of uniformity or even universality onto thought. I am merely saying, it is not personal. And from this it follows that there exists nothing personal, because the entire world is conceptual, it exists only within our thought. Abstractions of personality are false; they are conceptual, not actual. And they mislead and deceive us in keeping this division alive, for ever and ever. And the cause of sorrow, of all conflict, is this personalization of thought. If we really saw the impersonal nature of thought, then the thoughts would come and go; and we would let go of them, without resistance, without regrets. Conflict or sorrow may be here for a moment; exposed fully to attention in the Now, they would be seen one moment and be gone the next moment. But since we have personalized thought, we have a proprietary claim on certain thoughts and cannot let go of them. They come back to haunt us. We have vested interests, and that is the reason we try to control the thoughts. Thus, psychological suffering, which is entirely in and through thought, ever continues. Can you really understand that, fully, deeply?

V: If I did not have this brain, I would not have this thought.

RP: Leave the brain out of it. In some way it is a link, a switching station, in this process, but the essential thing is not to examine the brain, its physiological structure and all that, but to understand the psychological structure of thought—that is much more important.

V: The psychological structure of thought?

RP: Yes, which is the contents of consciousness. Consciousness is its contents. There is no duality. It is not: there is consciousness and I am filling it with thought. Please follow this a bit; it is very interesting. There is not the space and the mind's thoughts are filling the space of consciousness. And although that consciousness has evolved, there has never been a real transformation in it. Essentially, it has remained a consciousness of division, based on the personalization—the polarization of "me" and "not-me"—of thought, thus breeding conflict and sorrow.

V: And yet, the reason we accept this situation is that we find our identity in the thinking process. It is what makes it continue, keeps the whole thing going. Even though it is destructive, it is horrible and all that sort of thing, that is what I think I am. Then, how could I possibly extricate myself out of all that? That is what we have to question right now.

The thing I was trying to get into before is that our thought implies a thinker, the experience implies an experiencer, and thought is always moving in a sequential way. It always has a sense of continuity about it. So I feel my existence has continuity through my thought process. What we are examining now, the thought process that Robert has just actually described, is a purely mechanical, absolutely impersonal thing. It has nothing to do with the real self at all.

But we don't see it this way. Since we exist through the thinking process, we are loath to let go of it. Now if I see through all that, then perhaps the whole house of cards may begin to fall down. Then I don't have a vested interest in it anymore. I see it as absolutely impersonal, and not as myself at all. Going back to my old question, I don't think you are ever going to come to this, until at the same time you begin to question: If that is not myself, what *is* myself? But instead, what do I do? I go to another thought and redefine myself or reinvent myself in another way.

Second Visitor: But is it necessary to ask oneself that question, if one sees what one is not?

V: Yes, because the mind needs a permanence; it needs to know itself. It needs to find some order, a sense of knowing what it is. If you don't ask that question, you will go back into psychological thought. It is an absolute necessity. This question of identity is at the heart of all our activity. It is exactly what makes everything go just the way it is. I react my way according to the style of the identity that I found in my own thought about my self. So the answer to the question is what would break this whole thing open.

Second Visitor: But to see that, one sees that that is not really oneself. What you are saying is that one has to look what oneself really is.

V: Because otherwise, you will immediately buy the next thought.

Second Visitor: The question is how does one explore what one is?

V: He came very close inadvertently, when, in our last meeting, he asked that question about attention. He takes attention as a thought, as most of us do when we view attention as just another form of a mechanical, psychological process. But if I perceive attention as being the one factor which is not mechanical, the only thing that is outside of this whole chain of causation, and I also see that it is behind everything, behind all my mechanistic processes, that it is the base of everything—without awareness, without attention, there can't be any life, there can't be any thinking, there can't be anything at all—I then begin to suspect that that is the area, that is the place to look where my reality actually is.

RP: The very fact of seeing the chain of causality is marvelous. It implies that such seeing lies beyond causality. It is in the here and now. I see my enslavement and in the way of seeing it, I have introduced a new factor. Perceiving the frustration in my present activity, I realize I am frustrated because I want to achieve this or that, but something happens and it does not enable me to fulfil the wanted action. At that moment I see my whole past life acting out in the present moment, which is the source of all this misery—the whole business of having created that entity, that wants to have its way, the ego. In that act of pure seeing, there is no seer. Now that is it. There is a seeing, perceiving, but there is no seer, because there is no censor. And that is the beginning of freedom. And, most importantly, the crucial question of my real identity has resolved itself; and I am keenly aware that any verbal answer to it would be irrelevant. Have you ever come to that point, any of you?

V: You come to the stage where you know that the ultimate point is going to be mystery, period.

RP: But that is another thought, when you bring in the word "mystery." If you have seen clearly, there is no mystery at all. You see the whole process of time, which is thought. Then, whenever there is this attention, the same magic is there, because attention has a magic of its own that is timeless. There is nothing else; there is no center, you are the totality.

V: I don't know if this is relevant, about the term "peak experience." I think I only had one peak experience within my whole life. And that is when I was in a place called Esalen, and as a result of these discussions, similar to the present ones, about Gestalt and all that...

RP: Well, if you say "Gestalt," it is not similar; then it is conceptual.

V: I am in this hot tub and I am looking at the sky and the ocean and all these people, and at a particular second or moment I felt that I am one with everything.

RP: It can happen without Esalen; it can happen to any of us, even for no reason at all, purely accidentally.

V: And where do you go from there?

RP: It has no importance whatsoever. To attach importance to an experience, to get lost in that experience and wanting to go back to that, places you back once again into time. You see there is a vast misunderstanding about mysticism. I don't know if you have read any books on mysticism...they all try to arrive at an experience, some marvelous experience beyond this world. But it is totally irrelevant to what we are talking about.

It may be that there are all kinds of marvelous experiences—I am not denying that, I have had some myself—but I don't attach any value to them. The point is that we are not concerned with experience; what we are concerned with is understanding, insight, and to discover if there is a way of living in which one does not crave for experience, even peak experiences, because you don't need any of that. If you are already living in a mode that is fulfilment itself, then why should you be seeking for any peak experiences? Only a person who is incomplete and unfulfilled requires such an ecstasy. And in fact, it has been said the human brain is so delicate that it cannot continue living with ecstasy for very long. So these marvelous experiences can be another dead end, another way of losing sight of what is really important.

V: Because the experience is known...

RP: It is part of the known, exactly; immediately it becomes part of the known. It may be a high-grade experience, a marvelous one, or it may be a miserable one, but it is still experience, it is still as Alan said part of this whole chain of dream events.

V: It is already the past. And the extraordinary thing is this Now, because we keep underrating it. Every time I carry on about experience, I have diminished the notion of Now, and Now is the only depth there is. There is nothing beyond the Now. You can come to the most extraordinary experience, write it down and tell everyone about it, and if you would match that against the Now, it will never even get near. It is amazing, there is nothing that can compare with the Now. And yet thinking always underrates Now. Thinking is only interested in time, either the past experience or what I can do in the future. It is so utterly out of its element when it comes to the Now. Thinking is a movement just like time. Beingness, awareness, attention, is only concerned with Now and Nowness. It is perfectly enough for it just to be in the present. And so there exists this absolute contrast between the two things.

But I think there is another contrast in what you were saying before, this whole thing about abstraction, which is the essence of thought which is the movement of diminution, of making everything into smaller and smaller pieces. It is a matter of breaking up Nowness into something smaller. We have got this whole thing all mixed up, and it seems probably obvious to us now that the only way this can ever resolve itself is when thought ends by itself. Not me deciding to end thought. That is another thought. But if I see that the thought can only take me away from freedom, from what *is*, from being, from everything...thought is a very, very dangerous thing. It really is death. And when you have that feeling, you see it with attention, at that moment you are awake, you are alive, you are there. That is really where we are, right now.

RP: And that comes after death—that death in the Now. Death to all the memories, pleasant and unpleasant. After letting go of that, having seen the irrelevance of it, a human being can be truly free. And that freedom is through death only, after passing through the door of death. Then everything is transformed.

V: Psychological death you are speaking of?

RP: Of course. Dying to the old, to one's memories, to one's experiences, whether they were peak experiences or not.

V: To be absolutely in the Now, this moment.

RP: When there is death, there is no time. You are beyond time.

V: The capacity for thinking, however, after that experience is not lost?

RP: Naturally, thought is a valid tool wherever it is appropriate, and you don't lose that. You actually gain, because thought, psychologically, always interferes with our functioning, even on the technical level, as we have seen with the scientist. The scientist gets disturbing thoughts when the alluring idea of the Nobel Prize arises in him. That interferes with his actual scientific activities, so his work becomes less efficient, less intense, less creative. Once he has this ulterior motive, he is no longer free. But when you die to all these ulterior motives, then you are free to use thought in the most efficient manner.

V: Why don't we do this? Knowing all this about thought, its destructiveness, its irrelevance, the way it takes us from the Now, the way it keeps us in dreams and divides the whole world into pieces and creates all the problems, etc. Can you see why? This is what we tried to get at earlier. The reason why you won't buy this, even after Robert says it or you see it, and get it all clear in your mind, is because that is where we find our self. I find my identity in thought, and that is what we are trying to challenge tonight, to see clearly the absurdity of it, that that is *not* my identity. I think my identity lies in thought, and I have to see the trap I have set for myself. Now if that is not my identity, for Christ's sake, where is it? Unless I finally come to grips with that, I will always be subverted back into thought. No matter how much belief or disbelief you have about this process, you buy into it each time as long as you think that that is where you are. It is your safe place. And if this crazy guy can take that away, then what is left...and I am nowhere...then I have nothing left. That is the issue. I think this is the most important point we can come to, if you can stay with that.

RP: And every moment that you are in society, you are told the very opposite, you are told all the lies—that you have an identity, one which you must cultivate and defend, and that you should compete with others. So living in this society all the time, is the enemy.

V: But I have to live in this society.

RP: But you don't have to succumb to it! That is quite a difference. Now let's get this clear. You have to live in this society, we are not saying that you should go and live on some uninhabited island. I have never said any such thing; on the contrary, I have said: Live with what *is*. But if you don't understand what *is*, you are going to be kicked around and buried by it. Do you see that?

V: But if society had this concept of non-identity, we would not have the atom bomb, we would not have wars, we would not have communism, we would not be American, we would all be this completely universal identity. There would be no problems in society.

RP: But we are not dealing with society, we are not attacking society, we are not trying to reform society, we are dealing with each of us as individuals. Because that is the only way where we have access to the issue and the only thing about which we can do anything—the here-and-now "me"—and yet live in society with all this craziness going on. Live with craziness and remain sane!—that is the task. And it is very urgent, because the house is on fire and the world gets to be an increasingly dangerous place, for your physical as well as your psychological well-being. And because it is an accelerating process, and in view of the powerful means that scientists have made available to the leaders of nations, for the first time in history there is a distinct possibility that this earth as we know it will not continue. Mankind may be exterminated. See the urgency of all this! And see for yourselves that joining the anti-nuke movement won't make a bit of difference, essentially. The only difference there is, as Alan just said, is the seeing of the cause of this whole process of craziness, seeing the root of it within oneself, having constructed an identity where there is none. That is where it all flows from.

V: Yes, but if I don't join...

RP: Oh "yes, but!" [*laughter*]
You may join, it does not matter. There is no difference.

V: If nobody joins the anti-nuke, there will be all nukes.

RP: Not necessarily. See the root causes of all this and deal with these causes. Actually whether you join or not join is an issue on a different level that each of us has to work out. But it is more important to get a total perspective and to see the inevitability of all kinds of disastrous things happening, regardless of these protection movements. There is the hypnotic effect of that identity, that unreal thing that has such a tremendous power over us—it is a contradiction in words, actually, is it not?—but see the tremendous vitality it has, this false, non-existing entity; its power is beyond imagination. It is an evil power in a sense, if I may use that word without judgment. It is the power that can wreak havoc on everything, both in our personal lives and collectively on the national level. It is a power not to be joked with. It is more powerful than the energy contained within the atom. And until one comes to understand the source of that power, we are just playing around, dwelling on the surface.

Now there is a possibility of coming to grips with that power, but only by not being part of it. Be in a new consciousness by having clearly seen how the old consciousness is produced, how it ever perpetuates itself. And whenever one hears about a new consciousness, the old consciousness will immediately try to reduce it to its own level. Because that is a marvelous way to emasculate that vital new insight, and make it again into a thing of thought in which it will be totally devalued.

V: Once it is known, it already becomes a part of thought.

RP: It never becomes known, it is never known. That is why we were saying it is not that you or I know something and the others are just going to learn from it; the learning is in the Now without knowing anything; it is in a state of not-knowing.

V: That is no new consciousness.

RP: The new consciousness is the learning, it is that in the Now.

V: And that learning is in a dimension beyond thought?

RP: It is in a new dimension. Of course, it is. But do we all see the consequences on the worldly level—and I am not moaning about it, if the world is going to blow itself up, so let it, it purely had to happen—how this whole dark movement comes to fruition eventually. And it might end up in our destruction. So there is no point in saying, Oh how terrible!

V: One can apply the same thing to consciousness. Say, well

it is sort of an idealistic viewpoint, whatever will be will be, however I am, I am. Therefore, it does not matter.

RP: Of course, therefore, it does not matter. But you, do you want to live like that, yourself? Do you?

V: No.

RP: If you do, it is O.K.; don't say anymore. If you do, it is perfectly all right, too. And that is your fatedness, your state of understanding, your state of readiness at that particular moment. If you don't understand, and you say to yourself, it's O.K., let it happen, that is fine, too. And then there is the other person who has seen a glimmer of all this and has come to the realization that we live in a dream world. He has woken up momentarily, and he lives in the moment, and whenever he falls back into that dream state, he sees it. Or he does not see it. But whenever he perceives clearly, he does something to himself. Do you know what he does? He weakens the basic process of the false entity, and there is a change in that person. It must be. But there really has been no doing by himself; it has been a spontaneous change, in spite of himself.

V: But there is no choice in that.

RP: No, there is no choice in that. It is a seeing without choice.

V: One cannot choose whether it goes this way.

RP: It is not a conscious action. It happens by itself. It is an action by the moment, not by any entity. It is an action by life itself.

V: So the choice is an illusion.

RP: As you said earlier. It is a giving over to life. As long as I am intent on something, for instance on getting enlightenment, which again is a nebulous concept—I never like to use that word "enlightenment," because it gets one into hot water—nothing can happen. But if I give over and die to all that...

V: An act of surrender.

RP: I surrender. Then there is a chance for something to flower, from a new dimension in which my wishes, my efforts, are seen to be extremely paltry and totally irrelevant. And it just happens—in spite of me.

V: Do you like the term "awareness"? I become aware.

RP: You *are* aware. Not becoming, but in that moment, from moment to moment.

V: The term which you were using previously, the "reactive mind," comes from another religion. Do you know that it comes from a religion?

RP: I don't know. I just coined that word. I had never heard it before.

V: Oh, it has been coined by Ron Hubbard in Scientology.

RP: So I am in bad company then! [*laughter*]

V: Bad company?

RP: Well, I can't say I am in good company! [*laughter*]

So I think we had at least a lively discussion. Do you think these meetings have any point? Because we have to examine that, too. They are very pleasant and all that, there is a social aspect...

V: But if I say they have a point, then that is pointless.

RP: What do you mean by pointless? Now what I am trying to say is that really if one gets something out of these meetings, the stage may be reached that you feel they are pointless to you, as a person, because you have seen something, you have gained all that you are capable of gaining from this interaction and discussion, and you have become self-reliant. Again "self-reliant" is an inadequate term, because we don't know what self is. But there is something that has taken root and it matures in you; it is a maturing without being dependent any longer on meeting and discussing with others.

V: I don't think we are dependent on the meetings.

RP: Good, good, that is what I am getting at.

V: It is just that it is very nice meeting here. [*laughter*]

RP: But the time may come that one has done this sufficiently. And one may continue with it but there does not seem to be any more point to it.

V: Each individual has to see that for himself.

RP: Exactly.

V: You mean when I gain the insight, discover who I am, the meetings are not relevant anymore?

RP: They may be relevant, but not necessary. Some of us feel that we need this interchange at least initially, not because we are taking away from these meetings a lot of knowledge or information; on the contrary, we are leaving here totally empty-handed. But in the process, in the Now, in the moment of conversing and looking at things, something clicks.

V: Well, I feel it is still necessary for me, because I want to discuss things like what I read in astronomy, about the source of the universe—and that is irrelevant, of course.

RP: Well, there are lots of things that we could talk over—we could discuss such fascinating topics as space travel, black holes in the universe, the "Big Bang" theory, but there are many other, more appropriate venues for all those. And people who are much better qualified to guide such discussions than myself.

V: You would say that it is a meaningless question about the universe and what existed before the beginning?

RP: It is all conceptual, is it not? Because what is the point talking about the universe, when the universe is within you? And you don't know that "you." It is putting the cart before the horse, is it not?

I think this may be a fitting note on which to end this discussion.

6.

MAN'S ERRONEOUS SELF-CONCEPT IS THE CAUSE OF ALL MIND TURMOIL

Visitor: In several languages there are two distinct words for "knowing." One has the meaning of what I would tend to call crystallized, concrete knowledge, and which is more the cognitive level; the other you have to experience and the more you try to define it or catch hold of, the more it eludes you. The latter type of knowledge can be experienced or expressed in different mediums, like music, art, poetry and dance, or just in sitting still, meditating.

Robert Powell: First of all, we have the type of knowledge that is accumulative; it is the body of available information, of facts, theories, opinions—all that is knowledge, and we need some of this knowledge in order to survive on the physical plane. But there is also another kind of knowledge, which is here this moment and gone the next moment, because it is more of an insight than information, a seeing of how one functions, how the mind functions. It is a consciousness of the Now in the Now. And as documentation this type of knowledge is useless because the moment it is documented it becomes the accumulative, linear kind of knowledge. That is logical, isn't it?

V: But...I find this hard to say. You said something about knowing how the mind functions. I don't think that is necessarily what it is. To me, it is a knowing of existence, of being, it is an experience...I may not know how I am doing it. If I know how, I am in the other realm, the cognitive rather than what you call the Now. But I may or may not know how to do it.

RP: The cognitive way of knowing, that which is based on information, is always dualistic, needing an object and a subject. The object is in front of you and the subject is you as the cognizer. Your cognitive function serves as the subject and whatever else there is, whether it be a person, an inanimate object, or even a relationship, serves as the object. And always knowledge is within that relationship between object and subject. For example, when I say something about this table—that it is solid, has four legs, is brown, and so on—that is how I am expressing my knowledge about that object. This is one kind of knowledge.

The other kind of knowledge—and maybe we should not even call it that—is when I see in the moment without naming. For example, when I am angry, before even naming that feeling as such, there is a kind of contraction or fixation of the free-flowing energy, which is "me." I am energy, both bodily and mentally. And when anger takes place, there is only anger; there is not a person who is angry. At the very moment, when it starts, there is just that pure emotion of anger. Let us call it "experience" for a moment, although it is not a real experience, not yet. It only becomes experience in retrospect, when you name it. Now what happens when you do that? You can experience this for yourself: you are angry, right? This pure perception, this pure beingness in the state of anger...the mind comes in, looks at it and says "I am angry." Then, with that thought, a whole lot of associated thoughts enter. You may start saying to yourself, "I must not be angry." Or, "it is silly to be angry." Or, you may rationalize with: Yes, I am angry because...and then follow a whole lot of reasons.

So as soon as we have named anger, a stream of thoughts come in that try to work upon that innocent moment—innocent, because there is nothing wrong in having that particular sensation of anger; it does not need any kind of justification. It is what happens afterwards that causes our bonds to form—the conflict. And as soon as that happens, at that precise moment, duality starts.

I think we got as far as this in our last meeting. Alan was describing extensively what happens, how the thought gives rise to the thinker. Do you remember that? And he was saying what an incredible thing it is that duality comes into being at that particular point. And it is something very deep and subtle. We had just begun to mention this because it not quite as simple as it may seem. When duality comes in, it is really a strange kind of phenomenon, because the thinker is being formed immediately after the experience. But the thinker is not an entity; it is another thought, actually. It is a complex of thoughts and images.

Now, when you are angry, why should you rationalize your anger? Or why should you condemn your anger? This is very important, a very subtle point. It is because you have an image of yourself, and that image does not like to be associated with another image—that of anger.

V: But there is also the context of the social setting, where you may find yourself angry with the political situation or something like that. And since, as you said before, we are energy, we may make the conscious decision not to allow our energy to be expressed or to continue in that line of action.

RP: But who is that "we" who decides not to do this or that? You say, "we" decide to do this or that in the social context. But there is no "we," or if there is, we don't really know it; so you are begging the question. I say there is no "we" at all;

therefore, you are not allowed to use that word.

V: We have choices...

RP: No, we have no choices either. We went into that last time, you remember, the question of choice. You see, we cannot understand choice or how the thinker comes into being as the result of the thought, or any other topic within the spiritual area, in isolation. All these things are one in reality. And the mechanism of choice cannot be understood unless you understand the entity that exercises choice. Otherwise, we are going around in circles. That is what we are doing right now.

V: All right, I never expected all this...Are you saying then that everything is predestined?

RP: Everything body-mind does is predestined. Exactly.

V: Is that another word for "conditioned"?

RP: Predetermined. Cause and effect are at work. As we saw in our last meeting, our actions are always re-actions to what happened in the past and therefore there is no freedom. Every thought is the result of the past, of past memories.

V: But you are saying that as if it were bad.

RP: No, I am not saying that is bad, or in any judgmental way. I am simply stating that as a fact. I answered your question and Nathan's question. It is predetermined.

V: I believe it is predetermined.

RP: It is not belief, you have to see it.

V: Well, O.K., I partially see that.

RP: Ah, partially, is not good enough! You see or you don't see it.

V: I have seen it, because in the main I have been able to change my life. Now you may say, all that was in the cards anyway, but it wasn't; I really took some concrete steps to put myself next to other thoughts...so that I could grow or become the best person that I could be, or the most free.

RP: Until we really understand some of the basics, there should be no question of change...who is the "changer," the entity that changes? Who is the entity that "puts herself next to other thoughts," to keep to your phraseology? And "the other thoughts," are they any more free than the thoughts you had before? Or are all thoughts by their very nature unfree? Unless we come to absolutely intimate terms with this problem—who is the entity that does all these things, that makes choices, that strives to be free—until we know that, such so-called "change" will be a re-action to the old, a re-action from our present misunderstood situation. And we have already seen in past discussions that however much I try, I cannot escape that bondage of re-action.

V: It is part of being human.

RP: Yes, it is part of being human, but we are probing to see if it is possible to go beyond that condition. If you define the state of "being human" as being enslaved, and you are satisfied with that or resigned to it, I would say that is O.K. But if there is something within you that wants to go beyond the ordinary condition, something that may even have experienced such freedom on rare occasions, then if it comes down to using that term "choice," that is the only "choice" there is. And then again, that choice that we think we can make, it is not made by "us," but actually happens spontaneously when there is the insight into the mechanism of our bondage.

If you look at yourself and say, I am a human being with all the sorrow, all the conflict, and I will not seek for a way out, I feel that this is my condition, and I wholly accept it—that is all right, too. On the other hand, if you feel deeply within yourself that there must be another way because you have experienced some moments of freedom, of ecstasy, in which all this bondage was wiped out, this whole state of duality, and you felt yourself beyond; if you had a forefeeling or an intuition that there is another way of life, then something within you will quietly work towards an opening up in which the Other becomes possible. And that is the only choice there is. But it is not "choice" on the level of decision-making that we are faced with in everyday events, such as: Should I leave my husband or should I stay with him? That is a different kind of decision-making, because it is based on the chain of actions and re-actions.

V: But they are connected, I think.

RP: No, the two are wholly unconnected. They are in entirely different realms. The point is that I used the word "choice," and perhaps I should not have, because this may give rise to a semantic difficulty. The other choice I was talking about, whether you have this feeling of "earnestness," as Nisarga-datta Maharaj calls it, to seek the Other, to seek a different way of life, is not just an ordinary desire. It is a movement that already comes from the real self, from a deeper level of reality, and therefore it is debatable whether one should even call it "choice." However, I have called it that purposely, while fully aware of its limitations.

V: But what I was going to say is that oftentimes when I allow myself to accept the situation that I am in, or my circumstances, then I surrender to that. Then comes the "self." It is like when I stop trying to make something happen, I just resign myself either to the feeling that is there, or the circumstances, that I don't have any real control, and then all of a sudden, without even trying, it comes: this thing within me, which is striving for another way, and this flaying around or re-acting, disperses. Now I agree with you, there are those who don't allow the self to come up and who are hanging on to their misery or whatever, their re-activity. But I did not ask to be driven...it is the despair within me.

RP: We must be careful, though, when we use the word "accept" or "resign" that we are really accepting fully and not just partially, that we are not becoming stoics and rationalize our misfortune within the context of some philosophical theory and say: This is life's condition; we must accept, it is not given us to have all our wishes granted, and that kind of reasoning. You know the Greek philosophy of Stoicism, to be cool and self-collected under any circumstances, any misfortune; if it is that, it is no different from the ordinary way of action and re-action. Then we just try to make the best of it. To be in total acceptance is to be beyond any kind of thought, any kind of philosophy, any kind of rationalizing. It is an entirely different state.

Now only you can know in what state you are at any particular moment; that is up to you to see for yourself. But one must be aware that there are pitfalls, because the mind has an infinite capacity for self-deception. You must be prepared to lose your life, to die to everything—not just one or two little things. It is an all-or-nothing type of situation. That is what is called total let-go—letting go of the center.

V: I call that "faith."

RP: You may call it anything you like, but the word is not important. It is something one does or does not do. It is a tremendous thing. And it only happens when you can see through this whole process of what binds you, this process of unreality—the unreality that is us when we say "I" or "we."

As long as it is a reality to you, you are way off. You can talk about acceptance, resignation, let-go, but it has nothing whatsoever to do with the real let-go. Only when you can see totally through what you are...

V: Did you make the statement before that we can have an effect on other people without even trying? Or that this self is sometimes communicated even without us being conscious that that is going on? I believe that there is more of self in each one of us operating to a greater or lesser extent and it is not totally an all-or-nothing sort of situation...I think we need to strive for that.

RP: Strive for what? For being your own self? To strive for what you already are here and now, that seems absolutely unnecessary. You are the self, so why strive for it?

V: Well, the striving has more to do with the images that I have been given about myself by certain people that had I believed them would have been given up long ago.

RP: But who is the "striver"? Who is that entity?

V: It is the "I."

RP: It is another image. You are going around in circles again. You see how we do that? Unless we see this whole process of going around in circles, we are always begging the question.

V: But I prefer to think of it as a "spiral." [*laughter*]

RP: Call it a spiral, I don't mind. But "spiral" is a dangerous word, because spiralling implies evolution. It means not only do you go around in circles but you are also progressing, getting somewhere, and that is wholly untrue. That is what we would like to believe, that there is spiritual evolution, but these two words are mutually exclusive, since evolution is based on time and the world of the spirit is timeless.

V: You see, I agree with you on the one hand...

RP: Don't agree with me, please. Because the moment we say I agree or disagree, the self-examination stops.

V: I am in this body...

RP: Are you? I am sorry, but I am going to be very contrary this time. I am going to pick on everything she says! Just for the fun of it...I can quibble about that too, what you have just said. One has to go into all these issues, as we said before, the body, the mind, the self—the whole thing is inter-related. We pick on one topic, and end up somewhere entirely different. But all topics are basically the same. One must understand this whole question of who we are, first of all.

Who are we? What is our identity? We cannot even make such a statement as "I am in this body" without committing a serious error. Because we are not in this body, the body is in us. It is the total opposite.

V: I don't know.

RP: That is good. [*laughter*]

V: We started to explore the question, What is this "I"? in our last meeting. So, could we pursue this?

RP: Is there anyone who would like to bring up another topic for discussion?

V: I would like to talk a little more about predeterminism, because I have always held that the one thing that we are given is freedom. And as long as we live, we have this longing that goes with it.

RP: Were you here at the meeting before last?

V: No.

RP: Well, during that meeting we went into the whole question of free will. And what we were saying, very briefly, is that the free will-determinism antithesis is a long-standing problem that has never been solved within a philosophical context. And it will never be solved either, because the underlying premises are incorrect. You can never come to a conclusion, one way or another, intellectually. You cannot say, there is free will or there is determinism, or whatever, unless you understand this whole area that we are talking about. And if you understand it, you will arrive at an answer but that answer cannot be put into words. Nor is it a simple answer; it is not on that level at all. As we already stated, it can only be fruitfully approached if first one knows what one is. It is also logical; we are positing that the choice is between freedom and determinism. Freedom for what? Presumably, we are talking about an individual. Is the individual free or is he condemned to go through certain motions and he has no say in the matter whatsoever? So that is the issue. Now I say, don't bother about it within those terms of reference, that duality. First, go into yourself and find out what or who you are; then suddenly the whole issue will explode for you and everything will be crystal clear.

V: It becomes very complex when we begin the journey of exploration and realize that the "I" is the conditioned entity which is a disguise for reality, that that instrument is contaminated, and so the question is how can it be used on this journey?

RP: That is a very valid point you are raising, a very important one. It is basically the question: How does one explore? Does one explore according to a method, does one use knowledge, does one explore from a background, or does one do something entirely different? We have talked about this question of observing and listening, I think when Sarah was here before, and unless one has mastered that and understands it completely, this listening and seeing, there cannot be the right kind of exploration and therefore there cannot be any clarity in the end. Then that exploration would be mere introspection. Introspection is something entirely different; that is what the psychologists prescribe, because they start their journey of exploration with the assumption of an ego, an ego that has reality—not just relative but fundamental, independent reality. So the absoluteness of the ego is ever contained in their conclusion.

V: And the whole mission of the psychologists is to strengthen the ego.

RP: Naturally, that must happen. Their entire methodology is based upon the absolute reality of the ego, and in a way it is a kind of making the best of a bad job. We have this ego, they say, and it gives us all kinds of problems; so let us find a way of assuaging these problems, find a middle way. But it is not a radical solution at all, and our need is for radical measures to break our bondage and find the Other.

V: They are caught in the same myth.

RP: Yes, they are caught in that myth, exactly. So whatever flows from that premise is already contaminated. They have never properly gone into it, and they don't want to do so. For if they did, they would find that their whole science or art of psychology would be undermined and, consequently, their own importance.

V: But in a way, it is sort of happening by itself, this destruction of ego, I mean.

Second Visitor: Is it not because the individual is part of the problem—the individual, who is exploring the "I"? He has a vested interest there, also.

RP: Right, it is a self-defensive mechanism. If it is the individual who explores, he does not allow himself to find the total truth about himself. Because if he did, he would disappear. And he cannot disappear, for by definition the ego cannot let go of itself. The ego is an entity that will fight for its life, always.

V: It is usually led into it because of its own search and then becomes an authority that carries its own burden.

RP: Whatever it says, whatever it concludes, is begging the question. To "practice psychology" is already departing from a particular point of view—accepting and enclosing oneself within the reality of a "psyche" or mind and foreclosing any possibility of a realm beyond the mind.

V: The implication is that when one sees the falsity of one's ego, there is something else that we do not know that may be operating.

RP: Oh yes, but when you see the false as the false, then the real comes into being—at once and of its own will. Only in the denial of the false comes the real. The real cannot be approached positively. If you do, it becomes a projection.

V: I don't agree with that...

RP: Oh there she goes again, agreeing or disagreeing!

V: Well, because for *me*...

RP: For "me" means for *me*, too! If it is valid at all, it should be valid for all of us. There are no special conditions, there is nobody special here.

V: If I am doing it, holding off the negative, I am so focused in it...that the other can't happen. I need to...you see, I don't know the language to express myself, and you are making me feel insecure that I am going to...

RP: It is good to feel insecure, because we have to let go of our knowledge, of our security. That is a necessary part of this exploration, to be insecure. Because if you are secure, you are completely lost, and you are deceiving yourself. To be secure means "I know." Look, as we are going on with this exploration, I literally don't know anything. And I hope you don't either. This is true exploration: to look without any reference, beyond any frame of reference. I am trying to find out what you are saying, ascertain its truth or falsity. Because we are always on the level of thought, comparing notes, ideations, one concept with another, we ever stay on the level of concept. It is always based on the past, on memory, and when I am involved up to my neck in knowledge, which is the old consciousness, how can I ever find out anything new, that which is totally beyond thought, beyond the mind? I cannot. I am just extrapolating from the old, from my old consciousness. And then the result is still the old consciousness. If you perceive the process in its totality, and see the beauty of it, then the mind falls silent. That very perception makes me very quiet, because my mind, my ideations, theories, opinions, any agreements or disagreements with what others have said—I see that whole movement as totally useless, never leading to anything beyond itself. At that moment there is no more knowledge, there is only this vast emptiness, an emptiness in which I can start seeing things clearly without being burdened by information, by opinions, beliefs, and the corre-lations of concepts. Can you follow me a bit?

V: I experience it...as fulness.

RP: It is a fulness, definitely, not the usual emptiness of negation, of countering one thing with another. It is a total rebirth.

V: What I was going to say about this holding off, focusing on the negative, that in itself was even empowering me, whereas to let go of the insecure to go down into myself, I almost have to have a focus...

RP: No, don't have a focus, because if you have a focus, there must be a power behind it which focuses—that is con-centration. True meditation is the absence of concentration. Normally we concentrate, that is how the mind works. It is naturally dualistic, dualism being a process of exclusion. But if you are not excluding, then you find yourself in and as the whole. Isn't that right? Then you are everything. However, the mind is always acting like a concentrated beam of light, scanning. It is examining in piecemeal fashion; it cannot function otherwise. It is linear; thinking is a linear process, going from here to there, from the past to the future; or in space from this point to that point. It is never holistic.

V: It is best then not to think?

RP: You only think when you need to. Otherwise, it is best not to think, indeed. You need to think to do your job; on the material level, we need to think, otherwise you become moronic. But beyond that, we are always thinking; that is the whole point: our minds are never still. Be beyond the need for thinking.

V: When you meditate, you are not thinking.

RP: We are always spending energy in psychological movement. And that psychological movement creates the "me." It
is at once the ego. It is not that there is the ego on the one
hand and the psychological movement by an ego on the other
hand. The two are one process. And we always project
objects, because the "other" is also a form of energy. We
observe "it" or "him" or "her" as an object, from the various
preconceptions and conceptions that we have of that upon
which the mind focuses. And at the same time that we project and form an image in our mind of the other, in that very
same process we have made ourselves into subjectivity and
the other into an object. For example, I think of my father as
a father because I endow him with all the appropriate quali-
ties, I qualify him: he is my father, which brings a whole
world of thought into being. Fatherhood, you know, with all
its associations—he looks after me, he has authority over me,
he knows best or he may not know best, all that kind of
thought. Immediately I have done that, I am the son, I have
put myself into the role of a son. Otherwise, there is just this
consciousness, a unified field, but what we have now is two
images.

There is the image of the father, and my father has
accepted his image, because he has never examined it, and
perhaps it pleases him, so he is acting towards me in the
capacity of a "father"; and I am similarly acting towards him
as a "son," which is according to all the socially accepted
rules. And so that interaction of a father and son, what it
boils down to in actual fact, is an interaction between two
sets of images. And so everything in life proceeds on those
lines, because we are all acting out certain roles—the employer and the employee, the husband and wife, the guru and disciple—we are all in these various molds, always.

Society expects us to act in certain ways and if you don't,
then you are an oddball, aren't you?, or worse, you are an

outcast, you are a danger to that society. Naturally, if you don't conform, what is implied is that society might have to start examining itself or see the necessity thereof. It might begin to feel insecure about its foundation, and then you are considered to be a subversive. That is why the pressure to conform is so enormous. And we do conform, most of us, since we have never examined, we have accepted, all these roles, these artificialities. At the same time that the other has been projected by thought, one has fixed that energy, and one has made oneself into an object. Now when that whole process has come to an end, and one has dropped all these roles because their essential unreality or artificiality has been seen, only then is there something totally new, in which there is no duality: One is the infinite expanse of consciousness.

Thus, at this point, it is not a question of you letting go anymore, because there is no entity any longer that could let go. There is only the letting go. As long as there is an entity that lets go, it is a kind of mental acceptance, a stoic acceptance if you like, of one's plight. And it is a conscious, intentional action. But this thing we are referring to is totally beyond the mind. When you love somebody, when you do something with love in your heart, you just do it, do whatever comes up. If you think that you are doing it because you love, it is not love; then it is the mind at work.

V: What is the difference between caring and loving?

RP: They are totally different. I think we went into that during our previous meeting. Caring is still within the context of duality, however well intentioned it may be. And I am not against caring; caring is also necessary. But there is something much greater than caring. Love is of a different dimension. In love there is no entity that loves, and therefore there is no attachment, nor detachment. It is a spontaneous action.

V: I thought they were related, caring and loving.

Second Visitor: But when you care for people, you are doing something for them or think about them.

RP: Right, you are thinking about them, and that "thinking about" means a conceptual relationship in which the "other" is still separate from your self. Too often it implies a two-way traffic—a giving with the anticipation of receiving, although the latter part may well be wholly unconscious. You might call that a kind of caring. But loving is a giving without any anticipation of receiving. If there is an anticipation of receiving, then it is a trade, isn't it? I care for you, so long as you care for me. But the moment you stop caring for me, I stop caring for you. And that is when people talk about caring or loving. That is what they are referring to, without knowing, without really understanding it. They are using the terminology of love, but they mean something else: this kind of mutual dependency.

V: So love is choiceless.

RP: Yes, of course, without a center that chooses, timeless. But one cannot even talk about love; there is no point in it. It is a high-falutin concept for most of us, unless we understand ourselves. It is like putting the cart before the horse. There must be the right foundation, and love is not to be obtained by any means. It is not a matter of achieving.

V: It is much better to give than to receive, is it not?

RP: Love comes into being by itself—or it does not. We can go on describing love, giving definitions of it, but what is the point? Doing all that, you become very intellectual about it.

V: The reason why there are so many divorces is that everybody wants to get, not give in this society.

RP: But, you see, we have been brought up like that. Parents tell their daughters: find a husband, love him—that is all part of the old consciousness. And some are told a different set of stories about seeking a partner. The whole husband-wife relationship is a product of our conditioning.

V: They are not taught about themselves.

RP: But how can you teach a person about these matters?

V: You mean, as a parent?

RP: As a parent, or as a teacher. How can you teach a person to love? Love must flower by itself.

V: It must come from within.

RP: Indeed.

V: I believe children automatically love.

RP: Maybe, when they are very young, before being told about love.

V: Often one notices a certain smugness with people who say they have love. They profess to have all the answers to our social problems, and so on.

RP: Does not that smugness come immediately one has knowledge? I don't know the answer. As you were speaking, I was just trying to explore where the smugness comes from. And I wonder whether it is not intimately associated with the security that knowledge gives you. Knowledge is some kind of crutch upon which I rely, is it not? Because I feel threatened by the outside world, and I have been told "Knowledge is power."

V: It is a dangerous thing. Besides, it gives rise to pride. It is not a growing experience and it is not pleasant for other people who are trying to grow around it.

RP: You see, smugness and knowledge are part of the same problem, and they are based on the essential misconception of what I think I am, the idea of being a separate entity. As long as there is that insular being—and that is the way I have been brought up to believe, that I am "me" and you are somebody else, and that this whole humanity is actually cut up as individuals—so long as I believe that or accept it, there will be fear and insecurity.

V: I feel seeking security is a false search.

RP: I am asking whether it is necessary to have fear if one sees what one is. Where is the need for fear? I am asking a rhetorical question. For me, the question does not arise, because it is quite clear that from the state beyond the old consciousness, there is no such thing as fear any longer. But for the purpose of this discussion, purely pragmatically, I like to ask this question: Why should there be fear, when one sees the actual state of affairs?

V: As long as you are caught within thought, you are going to have fear. Fear is part of thought.

Second Visitor: Are you saying to us: Try to get your question right?

RP: Yes, and consequently nobody has given the right answer yet.

Fear is when there is an uncontrollable factor. We like to be in command of our lives. The possibility of something untoward happening is one major cause of fear, is it not? We cannot control things totally. It is a physical and psychological fact.

V: I think fear is a thief.

RP: Well now, having reduced it to the issue of to control or not to control, is it not a fact that so long as I am a separate entity, the question of control arises. Because that is the essence of duality. I wish for certain things to happen, and for certain other things not to happen to "me," as an independent entity. I want to control my life—control what will happen to me here and now and also in the future. And without this control, I fear the unknown—the force that controls events.

V: If there is no thought, there is no fear.

RP: Fear is a thought, so obviously without thought there is no fear. But I am asking something else. If you like, I will rephrase the question and say: Why does the thought come up, which contains fear? Is it not because I have made a basic assumption that certain things must happen and other things must not?

V: Well, that is from memory...

RP: Yes, it is from memory, but it is a fact that it happens.

V: Now that makes it a threat to comfort.

RP: Exactly, so I wish to remain as I am. I wish to retain the status quo in my life, basically, as a minimum condition. I may also want to enrich myself, aggrandize myself, improve myself. If I am fairly content with myself, I wish to maintain the status quo. And I cannot have the status quo for certain, because there are other entities, other forces, involved that may have a direct effect on my being. Therefore, I have the thought, the wish, of controlling the other—the non-"me"—in order to keep the "me" safe and secure, and carry on as usual.

V: So, if this is the reality, we need to pass through this purge of fear.

RP: You are going too fast, I am not there yet. I am still looking at it, exploring the situation. Right now, I am not interested in dealing with the fear. How does the fear come in? I see these enormous powers and forces beyond my little self. I realize I am very, very puny in this infinite world of entities and forces that actually or potentially all pose a threat to me, my current well-being. So I wish to keep them at bay. I say to myself, I wish they went away and left me alone. This is what we all do, essentially. Let everything happen, so long as nothing happens to me—me and my family, which is really an extension of the "me." Let everything happen, but keep me at least in a state of peace and tranquillity. And then, immediately associated with this situation, comes the idea of wanting to manipulate those people and forces around us, those circumstances, so that they will have no option but to leave me alone. And that is how this whole discussion arose about controlling things and events.

Sooner or later, but inevitably, the realization will dawn that the concept of control is a vain one and it is not possible to control the course of one's life in an absolute sense. Although there are people who appear to have acquired a certain power within their limited environment and have gotten away with a lot of things, who have not yet woken up to the fact that actually even they cannot control their lives, that ultimately there are circumstances and forces beyond their control...

Now if one really sees that, that in the end our fate is decided elsewhere, fear comes into being, because one never knows what tomorrow may bring. The "tomorrow" is the threat, not the today, the Now. Tomorrow I don't know what will happen when I wake up. My house may go up on fire, my wife may leave me, the whole world may go up in flames. I simply don't know because it belongs to the world of the unknown, and we are all afraid of the unknown.

Now a moment ago you were trying to say, and I interrupted you, that we must go beyond fear. But how can we go beyond fear so long as you stick to your conception of what you are? A conception which is erroneous, but if you believe it, if you truly believe that you are an island unto yourself, if you accept that and never question it, how can there ever be an end to fear? Because you will never be able to control what is going to happen to this little island. Can you see that?

V: I do, but I don't think in terms of this one being, which is one thing. There is also another dimension attached on a very personal, daily level; there is this little, itty-bitty "me" that is part of this larger extension, like a drop in the ocean.

RP: But the one is just like the other. You may look upon yourself as something extremely small or immensely large, as long as you have this conception of the "me" at all, and whatever is connected with it—your projected "me" may embrace the whole country, even the whole of humanity—as long as it is a projection from that "me," it is dualistic and, therefore, it is beyond control. This now really goes to the heart of the matter: How did this duality arise? And is there a way of finding oneself in—or bringing about—a different state, one of non-duality? This necessarily implies going beyond the mind, because the mind knows only how to project, whether it is starting from your country or your individual being, a big entity or a small entity, for essentially it wants security.

The mind wants absolute control, but it can never have it. If you can truly see that it can never have it, then there will be an end to the futile desire for control and self-protection, and thus to the movement of fear. If you can see that you are not an entity, have no limits, and that there are no divisions within you...

V: That is very dangerous thinking.

RP: It is not thinking, it is seeing. We are trying to apperceive things, dealing with facts, not projecting or philosophizing.

V: I have difficulty knowing my limits on a very practical basis. I don't even know how to say this.

RP: But is there anything to say? It is a fact, is it not, that as long as you stick to the conception which you have of yourself, as an entity, you are in a state of duality, and you are constantly threatened, because you have no control, you are in space and time and therefore you are vulnerable.

V: You are always in a state of fear.

RP: Always in the grips of fear. And it is no use to look for a condition of freedom from fear as long as you have that erroneous conception of yourself. But when I say "erroneous," I see it as such, but you must not just repeat what I am saying. You must work it out for yourselves, that is why you must not agree with me or disagree. You must come to see it as erroneous for yourself. To you it must be so, without any doubt. Then only the other can come into being.

Up to this point it has been a matter of philosophizing, opinion or speculation for you. But now see how that entity has come into being; this is the first thing. We have accepted that we are the way we are. You, as a person with all the images contained therein, that whole personhood or personality, the roles you play, we must see whether there is any reality in them or whether we have been indoctrinated, conditioned, and have accepted all these images, through habit, and fear too, through tradition, but all that from hearsay. Remember, there is a very powerful passage in *I Am That* in which Nisargadatta describes the predicament, the condition of human beings. They believe the most absurd things about themselves purely by hearsay. They like what others like, they fear what others fear; their lives and their dying are meaning-less. Can you remember that passage?

V: Do you believe that our lives are meaningless?

RP: It is not a matter of what I believe or not. I am trying to see what we are, how we live; and the way we live at the moment is a pitiful state. It has no meaning, simply because there is no freedom, because we are not authentic individuals. Because when that artificial identity that one has assumed—let us say in its simplest aspect, the identity of being a man or a woman—when that imposed identity of being male or female has disappeared, then the real man or woman manifests, and the real personality comes into being. Although the real self knows no multiplicity, and has no attributes, when reflected in space-time it has myriads of expressions, ranging from the grossest to the most refined. It is just like light, which in itself is invisible but only manifests itself when reflected by matter.

Is this a little too deep for most of us?

V: I feel it but I don't know what I feel.

RP: You feel it!

V: I am applying it. Of course, we are applying it according to what our faith is, in a way.

RP: No we are not applying it. If we apply it according to our faith, then you have a reference system of knowledge, and you are comparing my words with what you have heard somewhere else, and again you are stuck on authority. But if you see it for yourself as it is, clearly, it is not a question of what someone else has said and you accept that on faith, and you are comparing with what you hear now.

V: Is it possible that we could just get a glimpse of the oneness?

RP: We are that oneness.

V: We are not always aware of it.

RP: You are not allowing yourself; you are not open to it. You see, you are frightened, because you know that it means to be naked, to be defenseless, to let go of everything. And as long as one hangs on to that artificial personality, those marvelous roles we all play in society of being a "real man" or a "real woman," your authenticity as a human being is smothered, it is covered over by the mask. You know, personality comes from *persona*, meaning "mask." So that personality is really an artificial thing that we have acquired, that has been imposed on us.

V: But that is pointing to blame, we have taken the part.

RP: No, no, I am not blaming, I am describing the fact, the mechanism. Who is there to blame?

V: This condition of freedom is what brings, as you said in one of your talks, the feeling of joy.

RP: The two are inseparable— the freedom and joy or bliss.

V: You talk about this oneness with everything. Are you suggesting that we do not or should not have personality?

RP: I just told you. We have a real personality but it is not what you think you are. Let us approach it differently. First of all, it is rank speculation what you are engaged in right now. Because we have these personalities, we are burdened with them. And we see everything from this state of consciousness, through that personality. That personality is a kind of censor; it weighs everything it hears and sees, it judges and condemns.

V: I enjoy that.

RP: Likes and dislikes, leave them out for a moment. But watch how it bears out what has just been stated about the censor!

Now having all these masks—whether we enjoy the carnival or not—creates a problem. Imagine an actor on the stage. As long as he knows he is an actor, he just portrays a particular role, right? We are acting on the stage of life, but have forgotten that we are acting, we are so identified with our roles. So long as we have all these imposed roles, we have an imposed personality. Once that mask has fallen away, the real personality is unmasked and manifest. Because, if it were not so, you would be dead. You still have your creativity, which is uniquely, authentically expressed through that particular body. On the level of space-time, there is a manifestation. That is why the great spiritual masters who had liberated themselves from their own personalities, yet were each different, had an authenticity. Thus, Ramana Maharshi is different from Krishna Menon, who in turn is different from Nisargadatta Maharaj; they are not all of the same mold. Each of these liberated sages emanates something unique. The underlying truth is the same, but the expression is different; not fitting into any pattern, it is no longer a mechanical thing.

V: There is a difficulty in that we are seemingly enslaved by the "I"-identity, which does not allow us a moment of peace; the mind is in a continuous state of agitation. Yet, unless we have a still mind we can't go on to a different dimension.

RP: Yes, indeed. There are many of these double bind situations in life, and especially when you start confronting fundamental or spiritual issues. The whole thing can only be approached in its totality. Also, what we said earlier, you pick on one topic, try to get to the bottom of it, but that particular topic is associated with a host of others, which we have not explored yet. Therefore, one can only come to this through a holistic approach.

How does one start? One hears a lot about spirituality; you may pick up a little knowledge here and there and say to yourself, gee, that sounds real good; that sounds more truthful than the teaching I receive from my church, from my religion. But spirituality is something entirely different, and we don't know yet how to get into it. We don't know how to start. And I say the right way to start is to examine yourself, to be in a state of ongoing exploration, with total openness, without holding on to any prior knowledge, which means being beyond the intellect, beyond the mind.

V: But the investigation of oneself is beyond the intellect?

RP: Right. Just explore your desires; how they come into being, how they perpetuate themselves, surely that is not asking too much. Each of us can begin to do that.

V: Robert, when a person becomes serious in his introspective condition, then does humor escape? Where is the role of humor in all of this?

RP: A very important point, and I am glad you raised it. You know, the ego may pretend otherwise, but it cannot really be totally in a state of levity. The ego is always deadly serious, because it is insecure and on the defensive. Therefore, true humor escapes it, because it can only think of itself. And humor, essentially, is outside any pattern. That is why a situation may strike us as humorous, when it is merely something totally unexpected happening.

Humor is free from the pattern, and most of us function

in patterns. We thrive on repetition. Repeating is relying upon that with which we are familiar, which gives us security. So to be able to look at life without a prior pattern or precedent, is to be in a state of light-heartedness, to live with humor all the time. So to truly laugh at oneself, not as a gesture of false bravado but because one is truly viewing things from the totality, is only possible when you are no longer dominated by the seriousness, the lack of humor, of the ego. Humor is like music; it is a liberating factor, though it may last only a very short period or a split second. And, going back to what Nathan was saying, this exploration is like listening to music, or appreciating a humorous situation, because at that moment there are no demands from a centre. You are just pure looking itself, pure listening.

Going into the question of desire, how does it come about? You have a sensation, a perception, you see something that is beautiful, whether it be a physical object, a man, or a woman, and you want to possess it immediately. First there is sensation, contact, through perception, and you see the beauty of something, but it never stops there. Because immediately the mind comes in, and says, Ah, that's beautiful, that is desirable, I must have it, and you have created the object—you make yourself into a subject that wants to attain the object. There is no longer an act of pure perception; that is there only for a split second which is still on the level of nonduality. Immediately the mind comes in and says to itself, I like to have that, and so you have created the entity. You have created the subject that wants to attain the object. And if one is a little aware, you can catch yourself at that precise moment.

For instance, you see a beautiful car. Immediately thereafter, upon perception of the car, you see yourself in that car, which is the image you have of yourself in close association with the object. And it happens so quickly and is totally automatic, subconsciously, that you cannot control it. Even if you don't want to be enslaved, you have the hankering for that object, and you are hardly aware of the bondage it creates. Now awareness is being aware of one's thoughts, as they arise from moment to moment.

V: From what you are saying, it seems to me that true desire is the momentary awareness of the beauty of it...

RP: You mean, true perception, not desire.

V: Yes, and that one should stay within that perception, and not let it go beyond pure observation.

RP: No, I did not say that. You are creating another duality. You see this is what meditation is all about. We initially came here with the intention to talk about meditation, but now we have got into it accidentally. Meditation is just being passively aware of whatever transpires. As soon as you say, I should not desire, then you repress desire. And then the desire actually becomes stronger, because you have bottled it up. It is there within you. Like the monk who says, I must not look at a woman, because this will contaminate my pure soul. So he turns the other way, does not look. They do that, you know, in the East, where men are not supposed to look at women. Is he free from desire? No, of course, not. It is still there, deep within him, and much stronger, boiling, because he has not understood who or what is the entity that desires. Now as long as he does not understand, he will be tormented— possibly, for the rest of his life. And that is what all these ascetics are doing. They are suppressing; they are against pleasure. Sometimes they are even inflicting pain upon themselves purposefully, because they think by doing so they will acquire merit and get somewhere spiritually.

V: So what should he do then, the monk?

RP: I am describing what actually takes place. At issue is not what he should do or not do; he has been conditioned that way and does not know better.

V: But how can he release himself then, by knowing how to trigger...?

RP: No, no, you make it more difficult than it is. Simply stay with that observation, with the perception and with the desire arising. Stay with it. That is the liberating factor. But for that you have to see what it is that does the desiring. See the images immediately rushing into the picture, because there is no "me," no ego, actually. There are all these ideations, conceptual constructs, part linguistic and part imagery, that in their totality make up the ego. And they rush in at every desire. Whenever there is a desire or there is a fear, you have the interplay of all these constructs.

V: So he could just allow them to disperse naturally, these emotions, images...

RP: It is a transformation, not a dispersal. There is a big difference. It is not a transcendence either; we talk a lot about transcendence of desire, but this goes much deeper than that...

V: I don't understand...

RP: You should experience this. This is a thing that has to be experienced, otherwise it becomes book learning, an intellectual exercise.

V: Maybe, I thought, if I understood his problem, I could understand how to look at this sort of thing in my own situations.

RP: His problem is your problem, is my problem.

V: There is nothing he can do about it.

RP: Well, no, that is not it. It is not a question of he can or he can't do. Why do we say "he"? Let us say "I."

V: Because we are looking at the monk.

RP: Forget about the monk! [*laughter*] He is just an extreme example. To me, this is very vital, this whole business, because I know, I see, that if I can't understand this simple, basic situation of perception, desire and its aftermath, I am lost, totally lost. This is the ABC of it, the essence of my psychological functioning and condition. How does all this, this insidious conflict situation, come about? And will I be condemned for ever to function like this, in this mechanical fashion? Always re-acting in an inadequate manner, in such a way that I increase my enslavement. Because that is what I am doing essentially. Eventually, a moment arrives that I ask myself if there is another way of living altogether, in which I can be free from all this botheration.

If I, as Intelligence, in a state of pure witnessing, can see that anything done through the network of thought will lead only to further entanglement, isn't there then an immediate and spontaneous cessation of my habitual activity, a letting-go, in the same way that I drop a hot brick—without any thinking? And then at that very moment of non-interference, isn't there a realization that I am not that network of thought, that I am totally free of it? Thoughts may keep occurring to me, but I am no longer these thoughts, and that conceptual framework which is called "I" is not my self and it is therefore emasculated.

You must neither accept nor reject what I have said, but experiment with it—that is, if you are sufficiently interested. It is a vital issue, at least to me it is. And it should be to you, too, if you wish to live in a different way. Then you will have to come to terms with all this sooner or later.

7.

THE OLD CONSCIOUSNESS AND THE NEW—WAKING UP FROM LIFE'S DREAM

Public Talk at D.G. Wills' Bookstore, La Jolla, California, on the publication of The Blissful Life

ri Nisargadatta Maharaj, to my mind, is one of the outstanding spiritual teachers of all time. In many ways he is different from the usual Oriental guru. First of all, when I say "guru," that is already a highly loaded term replete with misleading associations. As you probably know, in the East they have a system in which the guru and his disciples stand in a very close relationship. It's not an entirely free relationship—and I'm using the word "guru" in the original sense, in the most established sense that we know—but a disciplinarian relationship. The disciple has to have complete obedience to his teacher, and also a kind of peculiar bonding between the two takes place. It's almost like parent and child—a symbiosis. Theirs is basically a relationship of dependency, psychological dependency, in which not only the student is dependent upon the teacher for his progress and well-being, but as you can gather, also the teacher, the guru, is dependent upon the disciple. Without disciples, the guru is not a guru. The teacher has put himself up in that particular role and gets some benefits too; therefore, such a relationship can easily turn into a form of mutual exploitation. Granted, this is the very worst picture I'm painting, but this is just so that you will have a realistic perspective on the matter. If you wish to pursue the subject more fully, I can recommend a book entitled *Godmen of India* by Peter Brent and published by Penguin Books (1972), which might prove helpful. Incidentally, Maharaj happens to be mentioned in this work whose main theme is the guru-disciple relationship. Most Westerners don't understand how strong and rigid that relationship can be.

Now, Maharaj is considered a guru, a teacher or master, but he is a guru not quite in the sense that I've just described. It is a little complicated and that's why I want to go into it with you to clear up this point. Maharaj actually belonged to a school of spiritual teachers, a tradition. I have described the details of it in my book, so if you are sufficiently interested you may want to look it up. Upon his guru's death, Maharaj became his successor and thereby the recognized teacher of that particular school, which was a school of *Advaita Vedanta*.

Advaita simply means non-duality, "not-two." And this teaching is based upon the traditional wisdom as given in the *Upanishads*. The *Upanishads* are probably the oldest spiritual teaching known to mankind, some three thousand years old or more. Originally an oral teaching, it was transmitted by word of mouth and written down only much later. And Maharaj was one of the most prominent modern teachers in that tradition.

There is another aspect to all this that is most important to understand. When I say that Maharaj was a teacher of the traditional wisdom, I must immediately add that he himself was totally indifferent to the whole guru system; he tolerated it because he found himself in an environment where it was the accepted thing, but essentially it didn't mean a darn thing to him! Moreover, he spoke exclusively from his own discovery, his own understanding, and he had never even studied the *Upanishads*. And I think it is a hallmark of the truly enlightened sage, of a true spiritual master, that his teaching, his whole being, is totally authentic; it is not derived from any other source than from within himself. Again, this is terribly important to understand. So although we talk about a teacher of the traditional wisdom, a master like Maharaj is totally against every form of tradition, since tradition is based upon the past, it entails the passing on of knowledge—information basically. What *advaita* is all about has nothing whatsoever to do with knowledge; it refers only to understanding, the discovery of what one is, one's identity, which is primary to the understanding of everything else.

I could have talked a little bit more about Maharaj as a person, but in this context it is totally unimportant. One thing I will mention though: he was married, which is fairly unusual for a guru, and he was a businessman (Incidentally, the school of teachers that Maharaj belonged to were all householders.). He had a little shop where he sold so-called "bidis," a special type of Indian cigarettes. But that's all I want to say about this subject. Whenever people wanted to find out about his background he dismissed it and said it's of no importance whatsoever. And you will find out why this is so within the context of the teaching. Now it is a very difficult matter to give the essence of this man's teaching, because unlike that of most other spiritual masters, his teaching does not lend itself very well to be formalized, and at the same time it is too subtle and too deep. Although Maharaj talked for many, many years about innumerable aspects of living and spirituality, he never introduced any concepts. Or if he deals with concepts at all, it is on a strictly provisional basis; they are concepts of a very special kind that point to the elimination of all concepts, in the same way that one thorn can serve in the removal of another thorn from the flesh, after which both are to be eliminated.

All one can do is take one particular aspect of his teaching and go very deeply into it. Since all aspects are interconnected, one might get a handle on the teaching as a whole. This is because the teaching is really no different from life, and life is an infinity. You can't just grasp it in your hand and say "this is living, do this and don't do that, these are the rules to be happy, the rules to avoid suffering," it just doesn't work like that. There are many schools, many teachers, who want to make you believe that it is as simple as that and they will try to tell you that *they* know the answers to your problems; they can explain to you how to be free, how to be creative. Unfortunately, it isn't quite so simple. There are no answers to life's problems in the form of formulas, there are no blueprints for living. Yet if one wishes to go very far and very deep, one must make a beginning somewhere. So where does one start in all this? In this connection, this little book (*The Blissful Life*) is primarily intended as a signpost. I couldn't possibly do justice to Maharaj's teaching, since that would be presumptuous on my part. How does one start coming to grips and so appreciating Maharaj's sublime teaching? Essentially, it is something that needs to be discovered for oneself, it cannot be put on paper in the form of a theorem or doctrine; it's something that one realizes in one's life from moment to moment, and therefore it is totally different from knowledge as written down.

So the first aspect of the teaching, which is a good steppingstone to start with, is to see that learning in our present consciousness is understood as an accumulative process—acquiring knowledge and building upon it. It's the way we learn about the physical world. Take for example the body. Biologically, physiologically, we understand it through acquiring data, information...the workings of the heart, lungs, circulation, and so on. And this is how we approach everything in life. Now, we must have information, naturally, otherwise you can't function in this world, you would be totally helpless. You could not hold down a job if you didn't have the proper knowledge; this is as essential as tools. On that level you must have knowledge. But to live without conflict, to live as a free human being requires a totally different approach. If you follow a set of rules, a discipline, or rely on a certain spiritual technique or practice, what will happen is that you will be practicing that method, that technique for the rest of your life or until you tire of it or get bored with it. In the process, you may well think that you are making progress from your present state of unhappiness. You have the goal in mind of "in the end I'll be happy, I'll be liberated." And by doing that, you will be deceiving yourself, because your premise would be wrong.

One of our premises in looking at the world and ourselves in it is that we are separate entities. This is the way a child is indoctrinated. He is supposed to have a particular identity, and everyone else has his own. In this way, we have established the first basic split, the "you" and "me." Our parents tell us this, our teachers teach it to us, the whole of our culture presupposes this concept of basic duality to be true. It is constantly being reinforced, which gives rise to man's insidious sense of "self-consciousness." This leads us to not only ever being in conflict within ourselves, but also in conflict and competition with each other. Thus, the basic driving force in this society is to "better" oneself, to be different from the other guy, to climb, to always what we call "evolve," become a better person, which process necessarily implies the putting down of another. And we have never questioned this process. Having been so thoroughly indoctrinated, we have accepted it as a basic truth and the only right way to live.

So, essentially, it boils down to the question of human identity; how man looks upon himself and the world. We have accepted that we are this body, that we are this label, this name, and this whole background of our upbringing, our knowledge, the way we function in society, our beliefs, opinions—the whole complex of images that we carry with us; in its totality, this constitutes the personality or persona. Now Maharaj destroys this erroneous conception of what we are totally, ruthlessly. Let me read you how he describes man's predicament:

> ...how little he knows himself, how he takes the most absurd statements about himself for holy truth. He is told that he is the body, was born, will die, has parents, duties; learns to like what others like and fear what others fear. Totally a creature of heredity and society, he lives by memory and acts by habits. Ignorant of himself and his true interests, he pursues false aims and is always frustrated. His life and death are meaningless and painful, and there seems to be no way out.
>
> (*I Am That*, page 432)

Now to most people that would be quite a shocking statement to make, right? And yet, how true it is.

What I tried to do in this book (referring to *The Blissful Life*) is to do the near-impossible and distill some of the essence of the teaching. I have said here:

> The teaching may be likened to a flawless diamond, dazzling in its brilliance and clarity, which has innumerable facets each giving entrance to the central truth and each reflecting all the others.

Let us look at one of these facets through examining a segment of one of the taped conversations with Maharaj:

> **Maharaj:** To know that you are neither body nor mind, watch yourself steadily and live unaffected by your body and mind, completely aloof, as if you were dead. It means you have no vested interests either in the body or in the mind.

Questioner: Dangerous!

Maharaj: I am not asking you to commit suicide nor can you. You can only kill the body. You cannot stop the mental process nor can you put an end to the person you think you are. Just remain unaffected. This complete aloofness unconcerned with mind and body is the best proof that at the core of your being, you are neither mind nor body. What happens to the mind and body may not be within your power to change, but you can always put an end to your imagining yourself to be the body and mind. Whatever happens remind yourself that only your body and mind are affected, not your self. The more earnest you are at remembering what needs to be remembered the sooner you will be aware of yourself as you are, for memory will become experience. Earnestness reveals being. What is imagined and willed becomes actuality. Here lies the danger as well as the way out.

Maharaj is referring here to the meditative state in which one looks at all one's thoughts, emotions, motivations—this continuous film of the thought process which plays before one's mind. Just to be quietly watching is not the kind of introspection that most people think it is, because in introspection there is an entity, a censor, an analyzer in other words, who mentates: "I see that I'm doing foolish things, I mustn't be foolish, I must do the opposite." Or, "I see my badness here and therefore I must try to be good." The latter represents the conventional, dualistic way of looking at things.

What Maharaj is talking about is nothing of the sort. He is referring to a state of choiceless or disinterested awareness in which one is totally the observer. There is a big difference:

a totally, fundamentally different approach. And when you see that process, all that mental activity, in purely watching it there is no identification—that is the beauty of it. In fact, there is a clean dissociation from all that, a stepping out of one's usual state of consciousness. But as soon as you say, this must not be, or that is good and the other thing that I'm trying to achieve is far away and I must approximate myself to that ideal, then you are totally involved. Therefore, you are wedded to the old consciousness that always tries to manipulate things, always tries to change its own mental state; and you are totally caught in this network of thought. As long as you are involved in your mental process and regard yourself as the owner of this body and the owner of your mind, then you have not yet entered meditation, it's merely trying to massage your thought process, your mental being. You can never be free this way.

Questioner: Would he also say that transformation is becoming more fully who I am or more fully my being...?

RP: Yes, but *more* doesn't come into it. It is a dangerous word to use because "more" means gradualism, and Maharaj and all the great spiritual teachers of this wisdom have said that there is this consciousness that we know of, which I prefer to call the old consciousness because it has been going on for thousands of years, and there is the possibility of immediately stepping out of it, which is its transcendence, through an acausal and timeless event; that is, such a transformation can be neither induced nor prevented. Thus, even the word "transformation" is not fully appropriate since we are already the self, when this is understood as the totality, and no effort to change ourselves is necessary; we must only realize that fact and drop all erroneous ideas about this self—just as it is sufficient to recognize the rope for the rope that it is in actuality and realize as illusory its appearance as a snake. This means that first all knowledge to which I cling emotionally, my psychological memory in its entirety—not piecemeal or over a period of time—must be rejected. Only then do I pave the way for transcendence of the old consciousness and the emergence of the new.

There is no fragmentation in reality; it's one ocean of infinity, it is consciousness. Now, this we always are, we don't have to strive to attain it, but we're not aware of it because we are constantly in a state of duality, in conflict. We are everlastingly trying to attain something, not awakened to it that we are that already. And that is what the title of Nisargadatta's masterwork is pointing to: I am That. The "That" has no duality and therefore is beyond space and time.

Thus, it's a matter of being wholly in the old consciousness or wholly in the other state, which may not even be a "state." Some actually call it a non-state, since it is totally beyond space-time: it is Stillness itself. There is no psychological activity. It doesn't mean that you become moronic, that you have lost your mind, not at all. But it is a condition in which thought knows its place and is activated only whenever it's appropriate, whenever needed. And most of us are totally lost in thought, immersed in it. We use thought all the time, we cannot be without it, never know what it is to be still.

Let us recapitulate here. The thought that originally was applied to knowledge of the world, this learning process which is based on information, and the correlation of all these various data and the building upon them, is basically the scientific, the technological approach to life. We need that since it is the way of what is called "progress" and even for physical survival. But that approach is totally different and has nothing in common with the insight into what one *is*, which is instantaneous.

Q:...since we need to deal with life as it is, we need to do these other things...

RP: Don't make it into another duality. If one lives from that insight that one is not what one appears to be, there are no more problems. You don't have to carry these compartments with you and say "this is knowledge of the technological world which I need" and "there I mustn't use my thought process." It does not work like that. There is something entirely different which one cannot describe; it cannot be expressed in words, but the nearest one comes to it is by saying that from the other state there is a creative activity, a movement that can deal adequately with the requirements of the moment. I would like to put it that way. These requirements will be met but the difference is that they are no longer met by an individual, an entity; everything happens by itself. This is, after all, the essence of spontaneity. But as long as you have this ego, which is a kind of neurotic thing really—basically it is the product of ignorance, ignorance about what we are—there cannot be true spontaneity. Occasionally, there are moments one experiences a genuine feeling of freedom and one does something on the spur of the moment...maybe it's because there is a feeling of genuine love, either for a person or for an object, or for an activity, and in that moment you lose yourself. But it never lasts; it's just a moment. Always you find yourself back in the old consciousness.

So in reality there is no duality at all. All one needs to do is to find out one's identity, and in the very finding of it the other may come into being. It's not a two-stage process, where I must first discover what I am, meditate and study and then come to a conclusion, and with that conclusion I am going to free myself. It's not like that at all. The whole thing happens in a flash, in the moment. You see your whole life, your whole misconception about yourself, and that's it. It is enough to totally see that misconception about one's identity, that I am not this body, not this shape with a label attached which reads Robert Powell, John Smith or whatever. I am not merely that sum total of roles that I am supposed to play in society, like being an American or a Russian; or being a professional man, a member of the middle class, a white-or a blue-collar worker; or being a father, a son...that we think we have parents is essentially that: a thought, a mental structure. We have assigned certain roles to ourselves, and immediately, implicitly, we assign corresponding roles to others, and vice versa, like the parent and child, employer and employee...there are thousands of examples of relationships like this where we have taken this role-playing to the *n*th degree. It's like an actor on stage who has lost sight of the fact that he is on stage...he has taken it so seriously that he thinks that he is that role. He has taken it totally to heart. He may make a good actor but he has lost his freedom because of being confined within that role-playing. And we find ourselves in that very same situation.

Q: [*The questioner is a well-known psychologist*] I have recently been reading about Bodhidharma ripping off his eyelids. Maharaj seems to be very much like him. Ever awake...to me, that's horrifying, always open eyes!! And my initial sense from my ordinary perspective is: How agonizing! Always awake and always aware. I wonder if you could comment on that and especially from the point of view of calling your book "The Blissful Life"?

RP: Yes. Of course, this story about Bodhidharma is very likely apocryphal. Because, taken literally, it's meaningless and preposterous. It is obviously a metaphor, to emphasize the fact that we are asleep and need to be awakened.

You have speculated about how horrifying this state of being continually awake must be. To me, that's a strange inversion of the facts. Do we not realize how stressful our present condition is? How in the old consciousness the ego is ever on the defensive, ever on tenterhooks and ready to fight for its life? In the new consciousness, the state of having awakened to our real nature, there has been a merging in the totality. Who or what is there to be agonized? Thus, the new consciousness is actually a state of total relaxation, because the consciousness no longer has to support the artificial structure of the "individual." How could it be otherwise when it concerns our natural state, our ground state?

Presently we are living in a dream world so long as we hold to this erroneous conception about ourselves, this false identity, with its implied duality...there isn't time to go into the origin, the whole mechanical process of how all this has come about. But the fact is that we are caught, have accepted this mirage, this dream, as our world, and we function from that dream, always. There is no reality in our actions. They are dream actions. So there is only one thing that one can do and that is to wake up, to be aware that it *is* a dream; only then will you come out of it. If in your dream you get an intimation that you are dreaming, then you are already well on the way to waking up, both physically and psychologically. Our present discussion is an effort in that direction, to make us doubt the reality of our present vision.

Q: If all the energy is one energy in which each of us is a part...

RP: That's still the old when you say "a part"...there is no part...

Q: So Maharaj would not distinguish between a superior, a higher power, and each of us sort of imbibing from that...

RP: Then you strengthen the duality...as soon as you say there is a higher and a lower consciousness, that's what all the organized religions are saying, whether it be Christianity or Hinduism in its orthodox form. They all say that because it's an easy form of conceptualizing, of establishing their whole hierarchy or structure of the lower and the higher, with the middle man, the priest, who would tell people what to do and all that. It's a most dangerous thing...there is only what *is*. Only what is from moment to moment, then that eliminates everything. Can you see the beauty of that?

What is reality? It is the truth of what *is*, now. Not yesterday or tomorrow. It is always what is in the Now. It is being totally in the present. There is that consciousness only; that is the consciousness of being in the present, and that's all there is. Even when I have a thought about what I remember of something that happened yesterday, that thought still occurs to me *now*, so there is ever only the now. . . and the past never exists. Similarly, when the mind projects from its memory contents, then that is what we call "the future." Being a projection, it is a construction, a production.

Q: I want to know what is the "is-ness."

RP: "Is-ness" is here now, right now. What *is* is the perception and the thought that your mind has at any moment. When you have a desire in the present moment, there is the thought "I wish this to happen"...or, "I want to have this or that"...and in that moment...please follow this a bit, because it is very interesting, and gives a clue to many problems. You have a desire or a fear, it's a movement in the mind, and a form of fixation of the energy that we are. Bodily and mentally, we are energy, we are a form of energy. You might say there is the field of the body-energy and that of the mind-energy; and at first approximation they appear to be different, but essentially they are one field. We have separated the body and mind. So that's the first thing.

When the mind has a thought, there is just this thought, this perturbation, a fixation of the energy, either as desire or as fear. Then what happens? Immediately afterwards a center comes into being. It doesn't happen in the moment of having a thought, a thought of fear or desire...before you have put the word "desire" to it, it is just a fixation of that energy. But it doesn't stay there...what happens is that immediately thereafter the mind comes in...

Originally, it is a perturbation in consciousness, you may call it that, but by naming it as desire, fear, envy or whatever, I give continuity to it, I perpetuate it and give it more force. When you want to escape from your fear, you strengthen it. When you think about desire and what you are going to do about it, how to fulfill that desire, you strengthen it. But when you don't continue with it, there is just that atomic thought energy which will dissipate by itself. It is the naming and the censoring, the entire process of mentation, that comes in and lends additional energy to the chain of action and reaction.

There is another aspect to this. When I said the center comes in, you have the thought and afterwards the thinker. Most of us think there is a thinker who produces his thoughts; that is the conventional wisdom. But if you examine it more closely, you will find it is the other way around. There is the thought and immediately thereafter another phenomenon takes place. A "thinker" comes in who reacts with the original thought. Now the interesting thing is that that "thinker" is only another thought, or, more accurately, is made up of thoughts and memories and is therefore not truly "personal." In other words, the thinker as such does not actually exist but is a concept that has been accepted through lack of examination; it is the image one has of oneself.

For an illustration of the detailed mechanism of the process, look in your daily life. Something happens to you. For example, somebody insults you or humiliates you. Or somebody is nice to you, flatters you. You have that experience; there is the thought of what is happening to you. You are being given a boost or you are being put down. Immediately, there is a realization of that fact, but that is not all. We wish it could stop there, then life would go on; you would be unaffected, you would be free. But there is another thought that comes in that consists of the image you have of yourself—maybe it is noble, good, pure or maybe it is wicked or whatever. You have an image and the outside happening interacts with that image, and the image does not like what it hears or sees; it immediately rejects it. Or it likes it, feels flattered, has been made to feel good by it and so attracts the experience, but the whole thing is a shadow play, merely an interaction of images. And it is important to realize that the juxtapositioning of the images is a purely automatic, mechanical process, caused not by a controlling entity but through the inherent magnetic attraction or repulsion of the images themselves.

Now when I am aware of the moment when the thought comes up and aware that I carry images of myself which I always protect, always defend, or try to beautify, I stop it because I recognize the inanity of it, the emptiness of it. Semantic convenience makes me say here: "I stop it..." but actually: it stops, or awareness and its clarity arrests the process. Then at one moment there is this thought and the next moment is it is gone. And there is no duality, because duality comes in only through the conflict, from emphasizing this thought in particular and interacting, playing with it. But if I let the thought come and go, and it is not named and not interfered with, then it is merely a fixation of energy and it dissipates.

Q: The psychologist would say, it does not dissipate; it goes some place, probably into the unconscious or the subconscious; then I do become an unfree person, because I am behaving out of this subconscious.

RP: You see, the psychologist starts from the wrong basis. His methodology is founded upon the assumption that there really is a "person," an ego, that can be free, whereas what we are trying to point out is that the ego itself, which comprises both the conscious and the unconscious, is totally a composite of falseness and the source of all trouble; it alone destroys freedom and nothing else does. The ego is essentially that bundle of memories, in the form of images and concepts of our imagined identity. But when you go into yourself and see that you are not those memories of sensations, the memories that you carry in your mind, if you see that those are imposed upon you, and that what you are in actuality is something much larger, that cannot even be described, an infinity, that is consciousness, then the whole world is within you as appearance, as phenomenon. You see that you are not within the world, you are not a small entity in a very large world but that the very opposite is the case. The whole world of phenomena, entities, creatures, is within my consciousness, and that consciousness has no boundaries, no divisions; it is infinity itself. Maharaj sometimes calls it the "dynamic manifest."

Q: I am not Infinity, I am not God.

RP: If you want to equate God with Infinity, you are God. And then there is only God, if you want to use that word...but I use the term consciousness, because "God" has certain associations—as one who is very powerful and I am not powerful, and he can do things that I can't...you know this whole indoctrination.

Q: "Loving," "magnanimous," "goodness that is overflowing in each of us and in all of reality"...

RP: It is an invention, a projection by the mind.

Q: It feels good to me...

RP: Ah, yes, this "feeling good," that is how and why it came about in the first place!

Q: But there were a lot of other things that did not feel a bit good that also were...

RP: No, no...but go into the reasons, you have to pursue this a bit more deeply. The whole idea of the Godhead, how it came about originally through fear, fear of the unknown. Wanting to be protected, the super father figure...and that is how we have all this and never questioned it, we have accepted all that. And this is another form of duality, and so we live in fear of what God might do to us. Or we want God to protect us. We can see all these dynamics present within our being. Do you know what Maharaj says in this connection? That in order for God to exist, we must first postulate that *we* exist, because God exists only through us and because of us. If it were not for us, there would be no God, we would not know about God. It is our consciousness...consciousness is primary to everything. The whole world depends upon consciousness, which is us. We are everything without limit, and without divisions.

Q: How do we know that God is not all-consciousness?

RP: If you put it like that, then it is a semantic game you are playing.

Q: I don't think it is semantic play...

RP: Yes, if you say God is Infinity, is everything, and therefore equate it with the consciousness we have been talking about, then you just give that another label. I am not interested in labels because eventually even these must go...you *are* consciousness, there is no need even to say it. So all words and labels are really insignificant. The main thing is to realize what one truly is. Then one is silent, and one does not need to divide the universe into different forms, different beings, higher and lower...all kinds of hierarchies. Then from that realization everything springs...All real values flow from knowing what one is and seeing things in their true light. Not the way we have been deceived, fooled to accept this pseudo reality, which is only a dream. Once you wake up, and get rid of these erroneous ideas and see things as they are in actuality, everything falls into place. Then you can make a beginning and you can go very far because it is an endless journey, this discovery of what life is all about. There are many more aspects about the nature of our functioning, our living in duality, that become clear when you have gone beyond it. First you must go beyond; like everything else in life if you want to study something, if you want to understand it, you have to have the widest possible perspective, you must take a distance and not be personally involved. If you are involved at all, then you look at it from a particular viewpoint, a small corner of reality, your background, which is always restrictive. But when you are not involved with any of this, and you stand totally aloof, only then can you look at it objectively and clearly. Then there is an entirely different kind of looking. When you have no desire to reach God, no fear of God, no ideation whatsoever, you are in a state of not-knowing, because knowing, knowledge, is basically memory, information, whether it be of the atom or of God or the Devil...it is information. And these are all images...

Q: Well, the mystics' experience of God...is so tremendous, it is like nothing...the response is a never-ending "Oh!" and I can think that is the Eastern mystics' experience of God and the Western mystics' experience of whatever name you give to it...

RP: Please, talk only of your own experience; that only has value, not the experience of others. But now that you have brought up the subject of mysticism, there is one fundamental misunderstanding in general. Let me say this about "mysticism." Again we are dealing with words. As it is normally defined, the word denotes the search for an experience...a marvelous experience...of otherness, or of goodness...or maybe God, and while there are such things as experiences that one may have in the course of one's inner exploration, in themselves they are not really terribly important. If you think they are important, then what you are doing is you are creating another fixation, another binding to one's memory. You see, the experience comes and goes, as the experience is not in the Now—and when it is in the Now, without naming, it is just that...momentary—it has no lasting value. When you give it lasting value, you start to worship it, as a memory. This is essentially what our old consciousness is doing, ever acting and reacting from the past, and never being in the present.

Now, in my book of words, true mysticism is not the search for some experience—although that may well be incidental to it—but a transformation through realization. And what this is about is insight—insight into oneself, and I will go even one step further and say that it means simply insight into what *is*. This is because "oneself" comprises everything, since there is no difference between the inside and the outside, inside my skin and outside my skin, which is an artificial division created by sensation and thought.

Q: So it is more like union.

RP: Even the word "union" I am not too happy about, because union, as you will agree with me, still implies an integration of two or more parts. When you say "union," you will have to have different components to bring together. What I am alluding to is that all that matters is seeing the non-existence of the parts. That is wholeness, experiencing wholeness, when you see that the parts are unreal, the result of the discriminating mind, with its untold conceptualizations; in short, they are part of our dream. For example, the body that I have is merely a fairly constant pattern of impressions from my sense organs having been finally processed by my brain, and that pattern of sensations has become part of my thought process. So whenever I refer to my body I am merely referring to that sensation. But when I go beyond sensation—sensation being a reaction from my neurological sys-tem—is there still a "body"? The fact is that your body exists for you only when you think of it. When you do not think of the body and its activities, for all practical purposes your body does not exist. But when you direct your attention to it, through the subsequent thoughts the body comes into being. Similarly, in deep sleep you are not aware of your body nor your mind. If you are in the dream state, you are aware of yourself, of your mind and you might have an entirely differ-ent body, that is possible too. And this goes to show once again that thought fabricates this whole thing; it projects the body as well as the mind. They are constructions within thought. And if you can see the unreality of thought, the rela-tivity of it, its impermanent nature, then you are free, then you are the Absolute. Then you are That which underlies everything, without which there would be no thought, no experience, no sensation. It is like light; you cannot see with-out it and likewise without that awareness nothing can exist. So it is not a matter of union, of integrating mind and body. The expression may be a very pragmatic one for describing of what goes on, but if you do not go beyond the words, it can be very misleading.

Q: I understand myself to be experiencing the image of that inner condition, being in the old consciousness. That inner condition for me is one more item in the collection. Then I react to that, the way I imagine it is.

Second Questioner: I thought when he described being aware all the time, that there was a terror in that. And I am also having reactions to this image. And because of these habits of mine, though I might for a moment or for a hundred years place this inner condition in a mental category separate from everything else, even doing that, is still part of this...

RP: It is still part of the old consciousness. It is a projection from the old onto something that it does not know but to which it assigns a label and calls it the "other," or the "new" consciousness.

Q: So my question is: How can we possibly approach the topic even using the *neti-neti* strategy if to do so involves us in the net of the mind, or, perhaps better, the net of body-mind? Are we not even at this moment, excited as I may be, involved with an elaboration of something that is still in terms of the old consciousness?

RP: Not if you don't project. I think, most of us, when we are not really serious, hear about these things and react towards them in the old way. We either think that the speaker has found something for himself, and it is over there and you want to acquire that, and therefore you make that into another goal; or maybe you dismiss the whole thing and say, it is totally unrealistic, it has nothing to do with the real world. These are two typical attitudes. Now unfortunately or fortunately, what I am talking about *is* the real world, the *only* real world. And what people call the real world, is to me a projection, a concept from memory, not what is now, an actuality. And so long as this process takes place, of comparison, of analysis, of even talking about the old and the new consciousness, if it does not go deeper than that it will never give you an insight into what *is*. It will not bring you closer to that "beingness in the present." And, as we have said, the only thing we can do is to start with ourselves, as we are. We are confused, full of ideation, concepts...things that have been rammed down our throats. The one sensible thing we can do is to start there, and to perceive all these fantasies, all these imaginations, to look at them, not being involved with them, not try to get out of them but just observe and find out how they have come about; be aware of one's motives, one's desires, and from that awareness, things will happen. You cannot do anything about it. If you try to reach or grasp what you have heard here tonight, ask yourself the fundamental question, Who is it that is trying to grasp it? If you wish to grasp it, and say Oh, it is marvelous, I want to be enlightened, I want to be free, who is doing it? The old consciousness! You see you are caught, because the old consciousness will want to immediately corrupt this whole thing. Ego, by definition, has a vested interest in its survival. It will always fight for its life and not let go, and what is involved in this is a tremendous letting go, all our memories, all our cherished possessions—I don't necessarily mean of the material kind, but the emotional attachments because the images that we have of the ego are built up from all these attachments. And that's really all we have, that's all we are, and we think that to be happy we have to have things, more and more of them; we have to fulfill all these desires. We have to work towards them and what Maharaj is saying basically is that you can be happy without having more things, without having any thing, without striving towards such a state of possession. Happiness is your birthright. Bliss is what you are, what your self is. The essential nature of the self is bliss. And bliss can only be when all of that other thing that you are not has been rejected. Not rejected by you, but simply because it has left you. All the objects we cling to, if you try to dismiss them, intentionally turn away from them, like a monk who goes into seclusion, then they still lurk in the background. The fascination, the magnetism of the objects, is still there—all the attachments. But when the objects leave of their own good will, their own volition, then that's where the miracle starts.

Our mental activity occurs always within a subject-object relationship; we think that we need all these objects to be happy. That is the essential nature of desire, to possess objects and control relationships, objects in the broader sense, which includes not only physical objects but also persons; we want to possess persons. We think that it is necessary for our security. We must have these relationships that we can depend upon and control. So this entire activity is all within thought, which is our prison. And we think that through the fulfilment of our desire, we can experience bliss. But, as we can all see in real life, if you have a gratification of a desire, there is only momentary relief, the release of some tension, the tension which is called desire. It is just a moment, and in that moment there is a kind of bliss. But it never lasts, because immediately the mind will project another goal, another object that it must have, and so we are never in a thought-free state, because always thought will come in and produce more goals, more objects. Both attraction and repulsion with respect to objects and persons are purely the result of conditioning and imagination. In wanting another person, to possess him or her, that other person is also a projection from one's own mind. Whether it be your wife, your husband, or your child, we have created the other as an entity, but in actuality it is no different from the "me"—that is, it lies strictly within the latter's sphere of activity.

Did that clarify your question?

Q: No, it did not; it touched upon it. Give me some more time, I will ask it again.

RP: The underlying mechanism in your question is to find a method, a "how-to," and a "how-to" is always in thought, always through will, through intentional action. And what we are saying here is that we are trying to cut through all this by seeing that the "how-to" is actually part of the problem and that it does not work. We have to go beyond the object that we think we need for our satisfaction, beyond the subject-object relationship. And one can only do that by deeply going through every one of one's motives for action, one's desires. Not analyze them, but see the desire and the ultimate emptiness of this whole process. Only then will it spend itself, as it were.

Q: I was seeing our discussion about the other condition as partaking of the old consciousness and conclusive in that how to get out of it. And I understand now how the question of instrumentality sets up subjects and objects.

RP: Yes, yes, and as soon as we make it into that other consciousness, we forget what we are doing in our current, actual state of consciousness, we are already making that "otherness" into the "old," a matter of knowledge, a methodology of how to achieve that, the "other," as a goal, and we are lost again. So what is important is merely giving attention to what *is*, our current condition, which is all there is because the "other" is an idea, and as long as one has not experienced it, another concept. Then you are back into playing, as you said, within the network of thought. You make that network a bit deeper or broader, but when all is said and done, you are still within the current network, and still stuck to the thought, the desire and the fear. Above all, you have to see where it all wells up from. If you don't go to the source with the desire and the fear, nothing can happen; all this entails exploration, deep exploration.

Q:...and there is also some process.

RP: No, it is from moment to moment. It does not involve memory.

Q: Living without memory?

RP: The problem you are mentioning here is that it might be construed as "gradualism," as a process that takes time. I am saying it is moment to moment, it is in the timeless moment, because time is an illusion, time is memory. As we said, there is only the Now. So it is always in the Now that one is doing it, since we are not depending upon memory—memory being knowledge, the formula, the method; we are just looking, and in that looking, that observing, there is no observer. There is just observation. Or, you might say—it comes to the same thing—you are totally the observer. The observed is within you, is within and part of the observer. And then, at that moment you are free from time, and you are free from gradualism, because you have a perception in that very moment, without thought confusing the issue. So that is a different kind of learning than what we are used to, the learning, the exploration of science and technology which is building upon existing knowledge, bit by bit, linearly.

Q: Earlier you spoke of...if one asks, Who is the one...? it reminded me of Ramana Maharshi...Nisargadatta Maharaj, his teaching, does not appear to be terribly different from Ramana Maharshi's.

RP: As I said, all these teachers are teaching *advaita*, and it does not matter out of whose mouth it comes. Maharaj and Ramana, and there have been several others...

Q: I have not finished my question. Maharshi, as I understand it, asked: Who is the one who understands? And so on, infinitely into the past. That was his "how-to."

RP:...his approach. It is not a "how-to," nor an infinite regression. It is a seeing, a bringing you back to the source of everything. Who am I? Because as Maharaj has said, it derives from the one thing we can all agree about: I am. The next logical question then is: Who is? Or maybe it is better to ask, What is the I rather than Who is the I?, since the latter already implies some conceptual knowledge, the idea of a person being involved with that "I." What is it? And to see that what we think we are is erroneous. That is where the liberation springs from. Then, if you can see what you are *not*, you don't even have to ask the next question. For that is all you can know, the mind can only know what you are not. Now, after discarding everything that one is not, is anything left? Yes, purely Awareness or Consciousness, as the ultimate background to our perception; that is what we are, and this Awareness cannot and need not know itself, for it is our very sentience, the basis of all knowing. Knowing always needs a subject and an object, a duality. Awareness is complete in itself. Knowing is only on that level, the level of duality. So therefore the question cannot be answered in positive terms, the question "Who am I?" Even if I say to you, it is Consciousness, it is a mere label, a word; it has no significance unless you yourself have the insight. Then words fall away completely. When you are in that state, you *are* That. And if you are That, then why bother to define yourself? That is why it is said simply "I am That"—where "That" is not defined. It is too immense, beyond any definition. It is the same problem as stated in Zen: The eye that sees cannot see itself. This is another form of pointing to the non-duality of what *is*. The eye (the "I") that sees cannot see itself, which is obviously so.

Q: What does Maharaj say about Death?

RP: What he says about it is utterly different from what our conventional wisdom states, which is that we are born to die. Maharaj does not acknowledge that we are born, nor that we die. Only the body is born. Since we are not identical with the body, you are neither born nor do you die.

Q: But we do have this body for a certain time. Because if he says...if he talks about the body...

RP: There is a body...the body expires, but the question is What happens to *me*? That's what most people are interested to know. What happens after I die? And that question is always answered based upon the wrong assumptions of what we are, because if I am identified...if I am that body, then there is no doubt about it: I die. And then I can imagine all sorts of things; I can project various fantasies, about what will happen to me afterwards, but that is obviously a product of thought, either fear or wishful thinking...

Q: So does he say we go on?

RP: I fear you are not getting the point. If I never was born, then there is nothing that can die and I have existed and exist, timelessly. As I told you earlier, what I am, I might approximate by saying—I am trying to do the impossible, putting this into words—I am Infinite. I don't mean Infinite only in the sense of space, I also mean that in the sense of time. I am spaceless and timeless, I am beyond space and time. Space-time results from, and exists within, me; but I do not exist within space-time. Therefore, if I exist at all my self *is*, timelessly, that is all one can say. I am not born into this world, the world is born within me, into me; the body is born, appears to be born, and appears to die because even that is on the relative level. As one explores and understands more deeply, one also comes to the insight that the body does not exist in actuality. As I said earlier, the body is ultimately a memory, it is a relative truth, it is not an actual or final truth. It is an appearance, a deception by our mind-brain complex that we have this body. So, if I am not born, how can I die? I exist beyond birth and death. Only my body changes and the mind. But I am not the body or the mind, the mind being a collection of memories. If I have no memory, have total amnesia, there is no recollection of being a person. My personhood is totally dependent upon memory—take that away and it is wiped out, like in Alzheimer's Disease. Its basis is memory, essentially.

Q: I remember you but you may not remember me...

RP: Yes, when we say that colloquially, we are referring to bodies or personalities. Now the interesting thing is there is another personality, when the personality that we have in the old consciousness has been transcended. If the image of the man, as we now have it in our society, either the man or the woman, which is a mere image, if that has gone, then the real man, or the real woman, manifests itself. And that is your true personality, which is not the personality Society has imposed upon you and which you wear as a mask—you know, "persona" actually means mask. This true personality is not tied to, or derived from a particular body (when it would be merely "individuality"). Alternatively, one might say—which comes to the same thing—it is tied to all bodies. This personality is the eternal expression of the self into the manifest world. In this manifestation the soma serves as a channel so long as the individuality does not stand in the way, for individuality and true personality are ever mutually exclusive. And such expression being eternal, and therefore outside any time-base, is not dependent upon thought, memory, or concept, and so is utterly unpredictable to the mind. And this personality being totally free from any pattern, it cannot possibly be remembered or recognized. Does that answer your question?

Q: Sort of. Well, it brings me to another question and that is: I don't want to reject...

RP: Who is it that does not want to...Ask yourself...it is a very instructive process. Ask yourself the next question. You say, "I don't want to reject my body-mind"?

Q: Right.

RP: Then you have to find out who or what says it, the entity that does not want to reject.

Q: It is not "me" that says it, it is not my body that says it, not my mind that says it, it is not my memory that says it or my imagination, but my creativity, my intuition, my feelings, it is the total being, entity, that I am.

RP: Right, but you think you are that which you take that "I" or "yourself" for, which are all the images, the thoughts, the feelings, the desires? Which are all based upon memory, the past that wishes to persist. So ultimately it is still your memory that states it does not want to reject the body-mind sphere of operation. And that memory is itself nothing but an emanation of body-mind. If you can see that, then you are already free from it. You then recognize it as an artificial thing, a relative thing that is not easily surrendered however, because surrender virtually amounts to death. Yet such dying to the artificial past is the key to partaking of the real Now. It is necessary to die to all that one has thought, all that one has cherished; and most of us find that very, very difficult to do.

Q: Why? Why let go of the past? I like it. I enjoy it.

RP: In that case, there is no problem. Then continue clinging to the past, and try not to think of death that is going to take everything away from you. The problem is only...just take the next step...when duality comes into being. If you can truly say to yourself, I like it, I like this relativity, I like the dream, then I say fine, there is no problem, go on dreaming happily. But it is never quite like that, is it? We want the dream and we also want the "other," which we don't even know...because you hear someone talking about it, it does not necessarily make this meaningful to you. Somebody else has had this...and it looks like some experience which we have not had, so we must also have it. Therefore, we want the present state of affairs to continue, but we also want Liberation...because we have heard about that and it sounds good. Or it becomes a fashionable goal, like in the seventies when many people were searching for something strange, something mystical...Don't you see the bind, the double bind, that one puts oneself into, the terrible conflict?...

8.

The *Maya* Principle
and Consciousness

Robert Powell: I think one of the bad habits we have is to take the world too seriously—the "world" both in the physical and the psychological sense. We take things—objects and persons—as being absolutely real. But when one examines those phenomena, we find that they are ephemeral, that they are mere apparitions. And that which is a mere apparition cannot possibly be the real, the Eternal, because it is here today and gone tomorrow. I would like to call this truth the *Maya* principle: our tendency to be fooled, to see a snake in every rope that we encounter. And because of that *Maya* principle, we never get an inkling of what we are in our real nature—not as an apparition, as something that is born and that dies. I think, if one does any meditation at all, the prime task should be to rid ourselves of all illusions.

It has been said that we must get to know ourselves. But how does one do that? Is the self something that you can grasp, you can strive for and conquer, or it is to be approached in a much more subtle way? First of all, one should recognize the phenomena for what they are, as mere apparitions. Then, after one has done that, and if anything remains, that must be the real. And to me, that is the only sensible and valid approach. Before one does anything in the spiritual area, this surely must be the basis of it, the ABC. Now when one goes to meetings such as the present one, we are inclined to ask all kinds of questions. And if you watch carefully, you will see that people invariably ask the questions based on this *Maya* principle or rather the non-recognition of the *Maya* principle. They make lots of assumptions about themselves; they have knowledge from hearsay, that they are born, they will die, that they have a name, form and design, and their questions are from that point of view. Right?

And because these questions are based on that erroneous point of view, the answers must be equally erroneous. Thus, the whole discussion becomes an exercise in futility. So, first of all, one has to come to grips with this *Maya* principle, the seeing of a snake in every rope. Then, if one does that, one is invariably compelled to address the question of one's identity. What am I really? Am I this body, am I this mind? Or, is what I am something that cannot possibly be expressed in words? I think the answer is I cannot possibly think about it, because it is something totally "other" than that which can be grasped by any concept, by any language. Having come to this point where I am totally incapable of formulating that which I am, I can only be silent. And in that silence, I can be That which I really am. But as soon as I get carried away in formulating any truth about what I am, I am back in the world of concepts. I feel that any meditation to be at all worthwhile, should be dealing with this matter of *Maya*. Because through understanding of that only, can you understand what the real self is.

Normally, we are identified with the body and with a name, and we never have an inkling, we are never aware, that this complex of concepts and memories that we call the "me" is totally a product of the imagination. And if we can only get hold of that, that understanding of the falsity of the "I"-thought and the "I"-concept, if one can come to grips with that, there is nothing else to be done. So, the identification has come about for various reasons, because of our education, our conditioning, mostly though because of our lack of examination, the absence of meditation—in the true sense of self-exploration. We have a superficial view of our body and a superficial experience of the mind and the concepts that are associated with that mind, and we jump to the conclusion that we are that. In this way, we are that complex of opinions, memories, and concepts.

Now I don't know whether you have ever given all this any thought, any reflection. For example, have you ever reflected on the nature of the body with which we are identified? The body obviously is inert. It does not assert that it has a particular identity, but it is the mind that does. The mind that has come forth as a result of the body is a closed system. Whatever it concludes is based on its own being. So if that mind tells itself, yes this is "me," I can prove that that mind has a real existence, it is still based on its own unreality because one can ask to whom is that mind real? To whom is that ego real? The answer is, of course, only to itself. It is a closed system! It is an example of closed-circuit reasoning. What it amounts to is that the mind is merely telling itself something, that it is real. But such a statement has no basis at all. It has no grounding, it does not come from the source of reality, from the Absolute. Waking up to this closed-circuit reasoning invalidates the reality of that phoney ego, that phoney reality, exploding it even on the physical level.

When you look at the world as it is, the more you examine it, the more you will find that there is no independent validation for its existence. The only basis that it has is the mind. It is interesting that the world comes into being at the same time that the "I am-ness," the beingness, comes into being. As soon as you are conscious, the world is observed. And as soon as this consciousness leaves you, for example if you fall into a swoon or you are dreamlessly asleep, everything is gone. So always the "I-am-ness" and the world arise at the same time; the two are one.

Visitor: When asleep, when there is no sensory input, there is nothing.

RP: Is No-thing actually nothing, or is it something totally beyond our concepts?

V: That is right, we "language" everything.

RP: And if you say "No-thing," it means the opposite of "Something," so No-thing to me can only be a concept; because you cannot possibly imagine what is No-thing, since it is beyond our human experience. And if you go into it, perhaps there is no such thing as No-thing. It is a projection when you say the "absence of Reality." That is a pure projection by the brain from one concept to its opposite.

Thus, when you see yourself in this light, you get a different feeling about the world and yourself. If that self and the world are one, then also the separation between one individual and another is false. Likewise, the separation between life and death is gone, because that separation was based on the physical existence of the body and the consequent emanation of a mind from that body. At no time does my body/mind leave the world, because the two are one and so cannot be separated!

V: I try to visualize myself as a baby of just two days old. Now this, I guess, is just speculation, because I don't remember. Maybe, he does not have a sense of himself. I am in the crib and the world is out there. Maybe, his awareness is kind of mixed up a little. He is not really sure where his hand stops and the crib begins.

RP: He is purely a physiological automaton. Since the memory has not yet been developed, conceptualization is at a minimum. But it begins and in a year or so lots of memories will have been acquired. But remember, as Nisargadatta stated, what we are essentially is a product of the five elements. And Maharaj keeps emphasizing that. Now why does he give so much importance to that, the fact that we are nothing more than the product of the five elements and the three *gunas*, which are the three main attributes? Because going back to, reflecting upon, one's birth, one comes to a very lively realization of that empirical ego which is purely a machine, a psycho-physiological machine, of action and reaction, which has a life of its own. To emphasize its mechanistic nature, Maharaj has also called this ego-consciousness the "Chemical." And by identifying with it, all the troubles start.

V: What are the five elements?

RP: Earth, water, fire, air and ether (the latter in the sense of space, but not in any pre-Einsteinian sense of the word "ether").

V: What would be the difference in the quality of being between somebody like Nisargadatta and a newborn baby, who does not have the ego or "I," various concepts, and so on? Are they the same?

RP: They obviously cannot be the same, but there is a very great affinity between their states. As Maharaj himself has said, as a man grows older, he lets go of all that he has learned and accumulated, and so comes closer to the state of his birth. When the moment comes to die, he is there; he becomes like that little child who has not yet got any intellectual attachments.

V: The only difference is that he knows how to talk about it, is aware of himself.

RP: Well, obviously, he embodies that state of being, where one has cut through all these illusions and has seen things as they really are. One does not observe the world any longer through the *Maya* principle.

V: What is the *Maya* principle?

RP: The *Maya* principle is when one sees a snake in every rope. Overcoming it is essential for seeing the real.

V: Yes, I understand that. But why do you use that term *Maya*?

RP: Oh, merely because it is a well-accepted terminology in Oriental thinking, not only in Hinduism but also Buddhism, meaning roughly "delusion." Actually, it also means "to measure." That is an interesting thing, because measurement again is a form of delusion: when you measure anything, you first have to accept it as a discreet entity. You cannot measure anything if there is no separateness, if there are no entities. So you measure in space and time those separate entities.

V: Who is responsible for this mischief-making, the ego or the *Maya* principle?

RP: Look, you cannot say that *Maya* and ego/mind are separate principles. They both derive from the same source, namely a lack of purity in the mind. The mind equals *Maya*. In fact, in the literature it is said that the mind *is Maya*. Because, without the illusion, without the impurities, there is no mind. The mind is only thought. We are not talking about thought in the scientific or technical sense, but thought in the psychological sense, all the hang-ups we have, all the erroneous ideas, taking the nonsense for the real. That is the *Maya*. And therefore, the mind has problems—as fear, as conflicts, as attachments. And then it struggles to become detached, and that leads to further problems. The mind aspires to attain realization, as though realization were something far off and has to be grasped. And the mind has one other strange property: it refuses to deal with itself. It refuses to look into itself, because that would be a deadly threat to the mind, a threat of self-extermination.

The *Maya* principle is a most powerful force. Because the alternative is death. Death of the ego, which is the solution. You see, there is no in-between, no compromise. Any compromise is a continuation of that *Maya* principle.

V: It is interesting that in Zen, in the art of swordmanship, they are engaged in a highly destructive art, in which the aspirant also drops his ego. The beautiful way in which he is able to fence and slay the enemy is based on his dropping the ego.

RP: Yes, but there is one problem here; it is the way you are putting it. When you say, he drops the ego, who exactly is it that drops the ego? Please go into it. It is a very important point. Who is the entity? Can there be an entity that drops the ego?

Would anyone else like to comment?

V: I have trouble with our language. I drop my ego. Whose "I" can drop my ego? Because the language itself is structured around the ego. So as soon as we start talking about it and try to allude to that which is not the ego, we are stuck in the language, and it becomes immensely difficult to talk about.

RP: Talking about Zen, there was a Zen Master by the name of Bankei, and he compared this process of what our friend here suggested, that one should drop the ego, with washing off blood with blood. You see, the "dropper" is part of the problem, of that which he wishes to be dropped. It can't be done. For the "dropper" and the "droppee" are one and the same!

V: A hopeless case!

RP: A hopeless case, indeed, don't start it! Don't try!

Returning now to our original point of discussion, can we see that the whole world of objects and persons is equally a deception, if I take them for real? But if I regard them as phenomena, as apparitions, just as I watch a play on television and see the persons in it as artificial figures, only symbolizing real persons, then I am out of all this, this *Maya* principle.

V: It is just like the rope and the snake.

RP: Yes, you *have* to go through this. If you don't see the illusion, there is no "real" for you. You cannot come to the real in any other way. You need to see the illusory, both in the television set—that it is only a television—and in the perception we have of the world—that it is only a perception, a production, and not something concrete, apart from ourselves. In short, what we call the world is only an image, a concept. This is terribly important. Once you get the point of this, the question whether you still have to do meditation becomes a moot one—you may have preempted it—because this is what meditation should be all about. This is the only point in doing meditation! It is to see through one's own illusions; to see that what we are getting so excited about in the world is really Nothing.

V: Could you give some example what real, mature meditation would be so that what you are talking about is not misunderstood?

RP: Well, what we are doing now *is* meditation. We have been analyzing, examining what we observe in the world and ourselves; this is the real meditation. And to see to what extent there is validity, to what extent we should take this seriously and also to what extent we are identified with these various images and apparitions. The fact is, we are highly identified and because of this identification, we have all these attachments, and also the opposite—various repulsions, the many things we are trying to run away from. And this situation, in its operational dynamics, gives rise to all the turmoil in the mind. Because we want to wriggle through this chaotic world in such a way that we remain unscathed and our attachments are carefully preserved.

But if you have gone through this meditation or investigation, there are no more attachments and you don't require anything anymore. You don't want anything except the basic physical things needed for survival, and you don't need to give much importance to that. You take that in your stride. But all the psychological hang-ups, where are they now? They had to go, because if you see that what one had been chasing is unreal, you don't have to work on them any longer; you don't have to train yourself to detach...they have just disappeared into thin air, and you can live in freedom. This is the real meaning of freedom. Not a partial freedom, a freedom *from*, which must always be partial, e.g. a freedom from oppression, a freedom from want. Not that these issues should not be addressed, as human beings you should have those freedoms as well. But they are superseded, they are dwarfed by this basic freedom that one should have, which is the freedom not to be limited psychologically or spiritually— a freedom from one's dynamic, empirical self with its inherent disturbance.

V: You mentioned not to have any wants, to be free of all this, except for the very basic things...

RP: Yes, food, clothing and shelter.

V: And if something happens, the body dies.

RP: Yes, that is common sense, but even there you are not attached to that, because you know that your body is basically an apparition only. The whole problem has arisen with us through our identification. Once one is identified with body, then survival becomes a problem too—a psychological problem. But if you are not identified, there is no longer a psychological problem, it is only a factual, technical problem: how to get food, how to get clothing, how to get housing, how to keep warm, and it stays on that level; it does not clutter the mind. You want to live in a house, but you don't care whether you live in a million-dollar or in non-million dollar house. Then meditation may not even be necessary if you can come to grips with this: basically, the issue of reality and unreality, and how to keep them apart.

V: It sounds so simple!

RP: Oh, why make it complicated, when it *is* simple?

V: I can understand that concept, but to see it directly in our own lives, it is important to talk about it and not merely intellectually.

RP: This concerns something that normally we don't examine, isn't it? Normally we avoid the subject. How many books have you read that deal with this topic, how many lectures have you attended, how many spiritual meetings where they really went into this matter—the dissection of our observation of the world? What we are talking about here is normally a taboo subject.

V: There is a tremendous fear and, therefore, incentive to drop it.

Second Visitor: That is the ego, that is the brain, that is what I do. All the attachments, all the things that I am, and all the things that I was. I have had the experience, like a fluttering switch, but I will say this, the total freedom is only...but we are afraid of it, that is why I slipped back instantly, into the other.

RP: At least, you must have had something, a desire, to attract you to this, even if it means self-destruction.

V: Oh yes, even if it means self-destruction, exactly.

RP: And, because we have to also see clearly that there is this kind of choice. If you don't want to pursue this investigation, then it is just as well to forget about spirituality once and for all, never come to another meeting like this, and not read another book on the matter, because you are really wasting time. It is either this or that.

V: Seeing all this, and being warned about concepts and the intellect and the mind, and how tricky it is, yet, we can have a very extensive, clear idea of this whole subject and be satisfied with that; and that seems to be wise because we see the world is not real.

RP: You are still caught by the *Maya* principle. You know what happens there? The ego is so smart! It has partially seen something and has drawn away from it. Then it uses that to suit itself! By way of rationalization for its own actions. It is a bag of trickery.

V: We create a philosopher's ego and assume that. While we think we are on our way, we actually have fallen asleep again.

RP: Also, at first, it is very unnerving that you have no solid ground underfoot; everything has been taken away.

V: One thing I wondered about is: What is the value of living when the body keeps moving in this programmed manner? What is the value of experience at all? Why be here?

RP: Well, who is asking the question? The mind/body complex is asking that question about itself. It has no validity; it is the wrong question. And the experience is only burdensome if you take it seriously and you are identified. If you are not identified with that, it is not "you."

V: In the round of *Maya*, I can recognize certain things that are almost messages from the Real. There may be certain inspirations that come to us using the clothing of *Maya*.

RP: Yes, the dreamless sleep state is really the best example. Where are all your problems, where are all your identifications in that state? And yet you exist! In that state there is peace and happiness, and an absence of conflict; and yet you exist. This, to me, is the greatest intimation of that Absolute Beingness.

V: When you say, "and yet you exist," well gosh, when I am asleep like that I have no memory...so I would say, I did not exist, I was gone!

RP: If you did not exist then, you would not exist now! There is some irony in the fact that I have to point out that at no time during your lifetime did you not exist. For, the exponents of traditional Western philosophy often accuse the proponents of *advaita* of sophistry in trying to prove that man at any time does not really exist. Where these critics miss the point is that *advaita* never states that man does not exist, but only that he does not exist in the way he has accepted—that is, as a separate body-mind entity with a distinct form and design. Another point is that when you say, "I was not there, there was nothing," then you are back into the old trap of misperceiving Nothingness—thinking like the nihilists that

Nothingness is zero or absolute nothingness.

V: Right, I grant you that.

RP: You can't have it both ways.

V: No. But I mean it is the logical avenue, to follow that. Because when I think of myself, I am thinking of the ego, the mind; and when I try to think of what is not, there is no word for that, necessarily.

RP: There are words for it, in Sanskrit. They call it: *Parabrahman* or *Paramatman*. It means the Absolute state, the state before all states, including the sleep state; that which is not a "state of" something but has grounding only in itself.

V: Robert, the feeling that if I do not wake up from that sleep, which is a state...

RP: The trouble is that we do wake up! So that ego has only subsided.

V: The only time we are happy is when we are asleep! [*laughter*]

RP: Why can't we be awake and function as in that state of sleep?

V: The reality is the dream state?

RP: I am not talking about the dream state. I am talking about the blessedness of dreamless sleep in actual, active living. One does not exclude the other.

I know there is such a state in actuality. It has been described by Ramana Maharshi, and also I am talking from my own experience. I know it is possible, to be awake yet not totally in the sense that we are during the day, but being awake and have one's awareness and have all the benefits of that sleep state, be totally still.

V: What do you mean by totally still?

RP: Not a movement of thought.

V: Is there a way towards this state?

RP: It just happens.

When it first happened to me, I was totally surprised, totally nonplused.

One must begin with the most important area of our life, that which centers around our supposed identity, and not be taken in by all these delusions.

V: Everything around you screams at you, this is "you." But if you are totally in the other state, you still perform but you do not identify with things anymore.

And another aspect is the feeling that *you do* everything in this life. This is also wrong, things just happen.

RP: We are identified, we struggle, we reach for something beyond, and that is not the way. Because the struggle itself, paradoxically, the search for the other, keeps you more strongly tethered to what you are at the moment, in that state of *Maya*, illusion. But when you separate yourself from all that, you don't create an additional duality. This presupposes that you have understood that psycho-physiological entity, that it is part of the "I-am-ness," which has come upon that which has no name, design; it has been imposed on you by superimposition but you are not that. You are purely that which underlies it, the substrate. Then you let it go on, you observe it, but you are not trying to change it. By the lack of effort to change it, something will happen to that. It will exhaust itself.

V: For me, it works sometimes, but not if there is a powerful delusion, then I am trapped. All these nice concepts of non-identification, a bit of Gurdjieff, of Krishnamurti, do no good when it is like a stranglehold. *Maya* is that stranglehold.

RP: Well, then that should be your *sadhana*. Whenever it happens, go through this and ask yourself, who is the one who has got the problem. What is that entity that is so upset, so much in duality? And again and again, whenever it happens. There is no other way. For if you directly confront it by opposite action, you merely reinforce the whole process.

V: I think, sometimes we feel like challenging things.

RP: Who is doing the challenging?
The mind is caught and therefore it is looking in upon itself. It is only the mind that can liberate itself. The mind is its own prison and the mind only is its own liberator. As they say in Oriental literature, the mind gets more and more pure and so free from what are called the *vasanas* or innate tendencies. These are habitual reactions, and as the mind gets thinner and thinner, so to say—that is, less oppressive—there is more and more freedom, and there is an emasculation of the process of *Maya*.

V: So therefore, I see the false as out there and I will not react.

RP: You see the false as the false, and also your own connection to that. See it and that's enough. If one then goes on brooding over it, this means there is still something that is not clear. Some connection still exists with that which one has seen. But if seen clearly, it automatically vanishes.

Why is it not cleared totally in the first place? Is it because of partial seeing? Our conditioning is so strong and society tells you certain things; for example, that you must not resign yourself to injustice, so you work up a righteous indignation. Is it possible to work up an indignation without being personally damaged by it?

V: I feel that even if you are emotionally affected by it, that is a moment. You realize that it is only the conditioned being that is doing its thing again and you leave it alone. So it releases whatever energy there is until it is out, and that is it.

RP: First, you have to accept that things are as they are. We are usually trying to change things, the world, and it is highly uncommon to see the world as it is—to say: That's it, I don't have to change it, I don't want to change it. The world in a sense is perfect, it is all right.

V: So don't try to change anything.

Second Visitor: But then we are told that we are indifferent to injustice.

V: But that indifference, too, is perfectly all right the way it is. There is nothing you can do to be different. We are the only difference, that is another thing.

Second Visitor: If you are indifferent to injustice, the injustice will remain.

V: That is probably the way the world is; and there is nothing you can do to change it. The feeling that you can change it is part of the whole picture, is part of the illusion.

Second Visitor: It can also be said then that I have a feeling of indifference.

V: But all that is part of the whole picture. It's very difficult to see that.

RP: We are not advocating the status quo. The world is moving all the time. Your moving towards a better condition, less physical suffering, does not necessarily imply that your well being depends on that world. Because you are not that. You are not the world. You are not identified. But at the same time, it does not mean that you are sitting there in an ivory tower and you are totally isolated from all things. You are participating to the extent that you are a human being and related on that level. But in your innermost being it will not have the slightest effect on the outcome, and at the same time you are not dependent on the outcome. It is, as they say in the *Bhagavad Gita*, working without any expectation of the fruit from that labour, any rewards from your actions, and so an entirely different state of being. In fact, such a way of functioning becomes automatic, spontaneous and natural, once the realization of the false has taken place and the normal process of trying to survive as a psychological entity has come to an end.

Then what is happening to all that energy? No longer being channeled towards individual psychological satisfaction or survival, it is now used in an entirely different and creative way. You never know exactly in what way the energy is to be utilized. Because that energy is part of creation itself, not individual creation, but Creation—the Universal Creation. And one is part of it. Therefore, this whole argument about what to do or not to do in the way of social reform becomes academic. One's actions will be correct, they will be proper, once one is no longer contributing to self-deception, to the illusory processes of *Maya*. And that is what we should be interested in, not what might happen after I have realized myself.

V: When we are young, we are taught, conditioned, that we are separate, that we are an individual, we are given a name...everything kind of localizes, the world is out there and the body is here, and that is what my brain revolves around. It tends to focus on the world, and our self, our possessions, and on trying to keep alive and get more of the pleasurable things and less of the painful things. But then there is awareness that is empty of all that.

RP: There is the possibility of an awakening in the individual. Sometimes, even only questioning where our society, our culture, leads to, and the madness of it all, may act as a catalyst. And then an incipient interest in spirituality takes place, but people don't know how to firm this interest and be stabilized in it, because they are still strongly conditioned by the organized religions, by the many pseudo gurus, and the things they read in the newspapers and popular books; consequently, they get caught up in another trend—"pop-spirituality." However, it is noteworthy that in a very rich country, on a very highly developed level, there are a few people who have come to the recognition that the prevailing standards and values are not doing anything towards their fulfilment. And then sometimes a few very rich people who have got everything that they could possibly need or want, give it all up. And there are more than a few examples, especially in the East, of very highly placed officials, with plenty of privileges, who gave it all up to become some guru's disciple or devotee.

V: The awareness that is empty of all conditions...

RP: Don't try to describe it, analyze it. The moment that you see through this whole forest of concepts, you give up trying to give names to that which is qualitatively, fundamentally, different from any concept. You can only call it the "other." Because all that is the self. When there are no more divisions, what is left only is the fact of the self, and all is the self. And that self has no space-time. It is beyond space-time. Space-time only comes into being with *Maya*, with measurement, as we discussed earlier. *Maya* is when you measure the separateness of the world.

V: *Maya* also comes with comparison?

RP: *Maya is* comparison. Measurement is comparison. Because when you measure things, you have to have a yardstick.

V: So one could call measurement and comparison a delusion.

RP: That is why you cannot define one without the other; what, after all, is the yardstick for reality?

V: It is almost the Unknown, the Ungraspable.

Second Visitor: Somewhere I have seen it written about this idea of observation, witnessing, awareness and thought. It has been pointed out that the mind cannot do anything to escape from itself or undo itself. In a sense, self-observation varies. There is one part of the mind that watches another part, and that is all still within the mind. And then there is an awareness that is not of the mind, it is from somewhere else; the self observing the ego and whatever it is that passes through and is held as the real. I have a hard time with this, to know, to experience the difference between the self-observation that is a mental experience and genuine awareness of everything that is from the real self and does not pass away.

RP: You can experience it in yourself when you are watching the thoughts from your conditioning in the normally grosser state of the mind that most people possess. It is ever from the point of view of a body-mind, from a fragmentary point of view. When such a mind looks at an entity, it is a conditioned observation. It has opinion in it, a particular background, and "education"—conditioning. That is one kind of observation. This is the kind of mental activity that most people in the world engage in almost exclusively.

Now there is another kind of observation without that observer-background, when you no longer look at things from a body-mind point of view, and you watch and ask questions. It is a totally different state. Some people call it the witness state, but I don't think it matters what you call it. And it happens only when the mind is totally quiet, silent. As long as there is the slightest bit of agitation, there can be no witnessing proper. The result is still conditioned, functioning as one does from a certain point of view, on the basis of being male or female, belonging to a certain age group, having the outlook on life of one's peers, and so on.

V: In certain teachings, like Gurdjieff's, they talk about self-observation: watch yourself, study yourself, look at your thoughts, feelings, and so on. I get the sense that that is either creating an observing self or going into a part of the mind which is projecting that there is an awareness beyond that or in an entirely different domain. Then the observer thinks he is aware, when actually he is only activating another mental process.

RP: Right, it is an intellectual exercise. You see, if a person has not seen through all this, this *Maya*, can his observation be anything but conditioned? He may think he is free from conditioning, but the thought of being free from conditioning is not the same as freedom from conditioning. If you are thinking that you are free, there is something that guides your thought, your observation, that makes you into an entity, an observing center. If you say to yourself, I am observing free from the observer, you are still there as an observer, you are still very much there as a conditioned entity. It is all an intellectual game, a kind of self-deception. But when this witnessing happens, you are not aware of doing any witnessing!

It is a qualitatively different state of being.

V: Sometimes that first state assumes or pretends it is the second state, but it is not. It is really very involved, something that needs some kind of maturity.

RP: It *is* maturity. Not, some kind of. Maturity is seeing the false as the false, and therefore *being* the real. Because you cannot see the real. If you see the real, as it was said earlier, you see it as an observer. And the real cannot be observed because you are that. It is like the eye that sees but cannot see itself. The real, you can only *be*. If you see it, you have just created duality. Only the world can be seen, not that which lies beyond the world or prior to the world—that which has produced the world. As Nisargadatta Maharaj is saying, whatever you see is not real. And whatever you understand is not real. Most people think that when you understand something, fully understand it, that must be the real. He says, not so, even that is not the real. But the real is *that which makes it possible for you to understand*. That would be my definition of the real or the self, if you insist on a definition. You see the subtlety? You are that through which you know that you are. I am that I am. Can you follow this?

V: I am not sure. I have the sense that I am that I am.

RP: You are the totality, the Whole. Can you see the Whole? You can't see the Whole. If you see it, it is a fragment.

V: Would this be the answer to Jean Klein's question about inviting what he calls a "fore-feeling"? Maybe the whole purpose is to see not so much the objects, but what lies at the back of them, and so come to the "I am."

RP: Jean says the same thing: You are the totality. But this totality is not the integration of a lot of fragments. The totality is beyond integration, because if you summate a lot of fragments, it is still a fragment. Only, it is a bigger fragment! You see, the totality equals Infinity, and we all know that by adding numbers together, however enormous they may be, they can never add up to Infinity; it lies in a different dimension altogether.

V: But in a way, I don't know that I am the totality. The only way of knowing is from knowing there is a person who says I am not the totality.

RP: You are the totality, but you don't know it.

V: In my condition of *Maya* I can only know that kind of fragmentary stuff. But if I ever go into the totality, it will disappear. When I come out of it, I will know that I was in it. But I know that I am not, here and now.

Second Visitor: Right now, this whole idea of totality is like a concept from a book to me.

RP: That is the trouble with most of us. We hear these things and take them as concepts. So only if we have come to the stage of piercing all concepts, can one come to anything like realizing this.

V: It is a real subtle trap on a higher level.

RP: We must begin with the simple. There is nothing that you can take home from these meetings, because we have to deal with things in the here-and-now and see if something clicks. If you want to remember anything at all, then remember that you are not the body; you are neither the body nor the mind. Because from thinking that, all your delusions spring. All the troubles, all the miseries start from that particular identification. There is nothing wrong with the body;

there is nothing wrong with the mind. They don't live in the self, they don't give rise to suffering, but it is only the identification with the body, with the mind, that does.

V: The fear is of not being a person and not being in the world. Klein talks about grasping. Just to say the grasping is wrong, you should not do it and all that, does not help a lot. What is that psychic creature that I believe I am and why does it want to grasp? What is the actual nature of the grasping? Just to say we are a more universal entity, that does not mean a whole lot.

RP: That is why you should stay with, abide in, that "I-am-ness," that consciousness, and see how it has come about, how it has come upon you, and has done so as a fully determined entity. You did not ask for it. You did not ask to be born into this world. Just see that it is a mechanical thing, an automatic thing, that has come upon you. You are not that. It has come upon "you" and in due course you have started to say, I am that. And then you became involved in all the travails of that entity, which is the world of the false, of delusion or *Maya.* You have identified yourself with that. But once I can see it clearly as the purely mechanical thing which it is, with a life of its own—that is not mine—I can face all that without a twinge. Because where is Death under those circumstances? I am still what I am, what I was, and what I always will be. In my essential nature I am not touched by time. "I-am-ness" and all time-bound things have and will only come upon me, that's all.

Our knowledge, from the start, is all from hearsay. This has developed into various patterns, habits, conceptualizations, and images—images of what we are, what we think we are. And also the feedback we get from society, what society thinks we are. We are characterized, stereotyped, be it as male, female, as a member of a particular vocation, of the Caucasian race, a professional man, etc.—all that has been imposed upon us and we have readily absorbed it. Now in one blow, through the mere act of seeing, you have repudiated all that mental stuff that had been swallowed and digested. There is nothing else; and finally you see: I am not that. You know that it has a life of its own, but again you can say with conviction: I am not that; let it come, let it be born and let it die. Who cares?

Do you realize that it is most subversive what we are talking about? The most subversive truth! Because it undermines everything that society has built up so laboriously over eons.

V: It is anarchy, right? [*laughter*]

RP: Yes, but it is also the ultimate self-love! The love of what one is—what one is in reality. Not what one is as a societal product, a societal image. And if you are at all serious, I think it is vitally necessary to do this. You can see the various identifications one after the other. In the end, all that you hold dear will be taken away from you, because death is the universal leveler. There is the death of the entity. And all that you are building up throughout your life, and all that you hang on to, will be gone, absolutely finished. So why bother with it in the first place? Why cultivate it? Why not let it go?

V: It sounds so cynical! I understand. I understand exactly what you have examined. But it does sound so cynical. Indeed, why bother?

RP: Not cynical, but realistic, and to one who is dreaming, it is shocking, but also a call for awakening.

V: Yes, it is. And yet here we are, we are born, go to school, so much is expected of us. We are compelled to do these things, to make a living...

Second Visitor: You do all that because it is fine, let it go its own way. So you make a million dollars! Yes!

V: Hopefully, if we did not identify so much with it, if it were torn away from us, it would not do us a thing, and you go on to your next million! [*laughter*]

RP: Sri Nisargadatta Maharaj had his own unique outlook on beingness; he said "I-am-ness" is a cheat, sneaked upon us. If you were asked to enter your mother's womb, would you have agreed to it? [*laughter*]

V: Well, we can only say that it does happen, that we are born.

RP: What is born? Something is born. The body. You are not born, but with the body, the "I am," the consciousness is born.

V: And the moment the consciousness arises, plurality is there. Only in duality can you be conscious. So even that consciousness you are not. It appears on the body as the mind. For a certain time, the consciousness is there, and dwells in the body, and that is where the problem lies.

Second Visitor: So there is no consciousness before you are born? Is that what you are saying?

V: Yes, it appears at a particular time.

RP: It needs a body, the support of what Nisargadatta calls a food-body. It needs a physical basis, a form, in order to manifest. And Maharaj also talks about the vital force or *prana*, needed to make it all possible.

V: What is this force before it enters the body?

RP: It is universal. It is universally present; on birth it enters and on death it leaves the body.

V: So then it goes back to universal consciousness?

Second Visitor: Yes, something like that.

V: Maharaj also says that you should hold on to this idea that you are only the consciousness, not the body or the mind. But even the consciousness you are not. Eventually, you will go beyond that, he says. But this is the one thing you have to keep in mind, you are not the body, not the mind, but only consciousness.

Second Visitor: And that is easy to grasp.

V: If you do this consistently, a time may arise that there is a full view of what you really are.

RP: Yes, in first instance you are the consciousness, which, freed from body-mind attributes, is the universal consciousness. Once stabilized therein, one realizes it is still a time-bound state and ultimately one is not that either. But the consciousness represents you, as it were. I think Nisargadatta Maharaj described this consciousness as being something like an advertisement, an announcement, of your real being. Perhaps another analogy would be of the object and its shadow. The shadow ever accompanies the object that casts it; the two are inseparable, yet the object is not the shadow. Similarly, the consciousness foreshadows the Self, but the Self is not the consciousness. The manifest only points to the Unmanifest.

9.

THE ULTIMATE
HERESY

Robert Powell: One of the aspects of our life that was discussed in our last meeting was the general feeling, always in the background of our activities, of a lack of meaning, a lack of fulfilment in our existence. We had just started to talk about this, and maybe during this meeting all of us can go into it. We know this feeling of emptiness, lack of satisfaction, of being ever in a state of restlessness, trying to achieve something, never being content with what *is* and therefore utterly at rest, which is one of our big problems. And the way I see it, it is a symptom of the way we function. We function in this particular mode, because there is no real insight into what one is as a human being. Not what one is in one's societal role or profession—as a husband or wife, or doctor, nurse, lawyer—for all that we know only too well. But what one is in beingness, consciousness...and we are always in this state of disequilibrium, which is caused by the tension between what we think we are and what we want to be, this process of "becoming." So this is one aspect, one symptom as it were, of our ignorance, the fundamental ignorance of our beingness, which each of us has to go into and find the answer to for himself.

It is something nobody can tell you about, no book can instruct you in. Books can only give you hints; it must be your own investigation. So maybe we can discuss this matter, why we always have this feeling that something in our existence is lacking and must be fulfilled. Because all human beings are in this situation, whether they are rich or poor, highly successful or miserable social failures—it does not make any difference. The poor man who becomes rich, after he has his millions in the bank, will one day be faced with that nagging question "What is the meaning of all this?, I still don't feel fulfilled," if he has any sensitivity left, and then starts looking for something else. Perhaps he then becomes interested in spirituality, and instead of hotly pursuing material goods, he is now pursuing something elusive called "happiness," or "fulfilment," or "meaning in life." So we are all in the same boat.

You know, a child, a very young child, has not got this problem. He just lives and plays, but growing older, he acquires the same problem and becomes restless and in extreme cases, because of this aimless drifting—always seeking hither and thither to find some fulfilment—he becomes a delinquent. He has been contaminated by the society, the culture, in which he is brought up and so conditioned to search for some kind of satisfaction. Meaningfulness, to most of us, in the way of functioning, is satisfaction, isn't it? It is a kind of gratification. And we never suspect there is a mode of functioning that does not entail gratification at all, but is living in the present in such a concentrated manner that the future is completely out of it and also the past. This is the state Maharaj refers to as the "I am" state, which is totally in the Now. It is a state of purity, because there is just "I am," which has not yet been superimposed by "I am this" or "I am that." Is that clear or am I talking in a mystifying way? It is the state of the young infant, who is just himself and quite happy to play. He has yet no thoughts as to seeking for meaningfulness.

Visitor: [*The gentleman has been a member of the Da Avabhasa*

(Da Free John) community] The infant is not seeking yet, except to avoid pain and displeasure of some kind. His mother does not come, or the room is too cold or too hot, the light is too bright, or something like that. That is how he is learning, at that rudimentary stage, to begin to contract from his initial state. We are like this [*demonstrating with his hand*]— I prefer this form—like a fist tightly bound up, but the infant starts like that—open and radiant, happy. And life then sort of closes in on him, and he starts to contract more and more. So we have got to reverse this whole process, let go and open up, and become aware. We have to do this consciously, because the infant was reacting unconsciously, and...

RP: Instinctively, because at this early stage it is strictly physiological. He needs warmth, nutrients and so on, so it is a survival mechanism of the physiological organism.

V: That born condition is one of contraction—contraction away from this "All is one," happiness, joy and bliss: "I am cold, change my diapers," or something like that. And now we have to deliberately start discharging the things accumulated over decades, and that's what is the problem. I think we all have these intimations of which you have spoken, and what the great adepts have brought to us, from this prior condition so to speak. But we have not been able to rev ourselves up on that to a sufficient extent of discharge to get those fingers opened up. We tend to say we love our misery, we hug it to us—and it is ridiculous, of course, from a fully conscious point of view—but that is what we are doing. And so you've got to get on this way somewhere, this conscious process of releasing. It is also helpful to be in the company of the adepts and live with the great traditions and absorb all this and check ourselves. That is why living in a community is a good idea, because when you are with a bunch of people of more or less similar understanding, they can tell you when you are off base and you can tell them. So you can help each other to straighten up in one way or another. It is like a big family. Get rid of this ordinary, common society, which is just a mass of the old stuff and try to get to the new stuff, so to speak.

RP: But maybe such community living is making it too easy! For me, the ordinary society, the ordinary life, with no holds barred, is the best training school. From a spiritual point of view, the many shocks encountered in everyday life ought to be welcomed as a help in checking ourselves and not to be cushioned or pampered. Now to return to what we were discussing, one feature that the child displays in abundance is his capacity to play without turning it into serious business. I think that distinguishes him psychologically from the adult who finds it difficult to play just for the sake of play, without getting carried away by it and wanting more. The fact that we are aware of ourselves as creatures, as individual entities, is the seed for this process of "becoming."

V: The child, the infant, does not have that yet. It is only when that starts, that the problem arises. I am not sure that the child learns contraction, whether contraction is unnatural at that point. It is just a series of natural responses, and I don't think contraction is an issue there. But it becomes an issue later, and contraction becomes rooted psychologically, as he fights, defends, protects. But the thing that this activity tries to hang on to is this unfounded notion of being a separate entity. Somehow that idea becomes implanted in us, partly through society, partly because I think we have a predisposition towards it, perhaps inherently. Once that begins to blossom, everything else becomes a series of contractual defenses and resistances, and we end up back in the soup. And true "players" are unheard of after that, except in very rare moments. Even what we call players, the competitive, egotistical thing in sports and stuff like that, it is nothing like what the infant means by playing.

Second Visitor: No freedom here.

V: It is something like: "Me, I am good at it, I am winning, off with you, you are winning over me, and that makes me feel lousy..." that has nothing to do with play.

RP: It becomes an escapism, because one can't live with the emptiness or loneliness which is there immediately the creature becomes aware of himself as a separate entity. And that sets into motion this whole process of becoming. It is always an escape from what *is* by trying to attain something in the future, some ideal, some achievement, some goal. It is this general process of end-seeking, which characterizes our life style. And play is the very opposite; it is a "being in the here-and-now," a doing for the sake of doing, not for the sake of achieving, or results. In the *Bhagavad Gita*, they talk about action without fruits, do you remember? It is interesting to note that in our language the word "fruitless" has such a negative connotation, whereas from the point of view of spirituality it would refer to the highest form of activity.

V: Like "doing nothing," it is considered a crime.

RP: Wasting time! But, you know, there *is* no time to be wasted. [*laughter*] That is the beauty of it. For "time" is synonymous with becoming, isn't it? Psychological time. So to sum up what we have been discussing, we cannot break through on this problem of meaninglessness and this general feeling of unease or dis-ease that is always with us, if we have not first solved the problem of who or what we are. And as long as we are a social creature, there will always be this gnawing feeling of emptiness, however much we try to escape from it by endless activities. They may be the most noble activities or the most sordid, it does not matter; they are basically movements away from what one is, and therefore a danger. We are not meant to function in this way. This is man's way of functioning, this process of becoming; it is self-imposed. And to discover whether there is another way of functioning, with ease rather than with dis- or un-ease, we must go deeply into ourselves. This is almost a cliché, yet we always have to come back to this fact. We have a problem and we must throw it back at the entity who creates the problem. The problem-maker has to find out who or what he is. When he discovers that, the truth about himself, he also finds the truth about everything else, because everything is within that self. The whole world, the whole cosmos is within oneself, rather than what we normally take the truth to be: oneself within this enormous cosmos. This is the duality that we are being brought up with and have accepted, and we live it out every moment of our lives. And therefore we are always in fear, because when there is the "you" and the other—the "non-you"—the "you" wishes to protect itself against the uncertainties, against the threats from that "non-you." It is logical, isn't it? So there can never be peace, and the mind as it is, which is the cause of our misery, is just that interface, that state of friction, between the "me" and the "non-me." But when the two have merged, that mind has gone. Then there is the state of Nothingness, which comprises everything.

Would anyone like to make some further comments?

V: I was thinking as you were talking, in doing this there is something heretical in this whole thing. It would not matter what culture, what society one is in, this kind of thinking is very heretical. I found in the years that I have been thinking about it there is a lot of anxiety about going into this, because one is really rowing against the tide. Duality seems natural to the human condition; this other state does not. Any society, I would think, has some vested interest in the dualistic, western-type thinking. When I have internalized my society's standards, any time I make any inroads in that other direction I naturally am putting myself at odds with the way society thinks. You spend all these years becoming socialized in getting all the right stuff down only to find that the "right stuff" is exactly what prevents you from reaching the real!

RP: I am asking: Is there the individual, as apart from society, actually? And is there society apart from the individual? Or is that another one of our delusions? That is something one has to go into. To me, there is no individual apart from society. One needs the other, and they are one. We are collective beings, or you might say society is the projection by an individual who has misunderstood reality. Is that right, is it legitimate to say something like that?

V: Projection...What you said before, seems so utterly true. We are society, and society is us. And there is actually no difference whatsoever. The thing that fears upsetting society or being heretical to society, that too is society. There is nothing that is not this! The trick that the mind is always trying to play...it creates another division the moment the mind moves—left, right, center, in any direction—blaming society or whatever, it grasps the nearest symbol, the nearest thought, the nearest concept. And once it has got that, it again, as Robert says, has been another movement away from what *is*. It is the subtlest going around, really amazing...the contraction you spoke of is in so many subtle areas and so many subtle ways: we defend, fight, trick ourselves, play this and that game...the mind is either entertaining itself or rebuilding its image or keeping itself a little more pure and austere as opposed to society. But it is all a fraud, the whole thing!

I only understand psychological movements in terms of an individual self. That is the only way my mind seems to work, it functions only in that track. I don't trust any of it anymore; it is all the same process. There is no "better" mind and a "worse" mind; they are both part of the same movement. And at a certain point I come to see it starkly and that short-circuits the system, even only for a split moment. But you have to really see it clearly.

RP: In its totality. Usually what we do is we see something as an abstraction, in a contracted way, one might say. Our vision is part of the contraction; it is always colored by our basic assumptions whether they be conscious or unconscious. They are always based on being separate, just like most of our so-called spiritual activities—like all these groups that one sees especially in this part of the world, California—people who get together under the flag of religion or spirituality. You know what they are basically concerned with? To give some kind of legitimacy for that individuality, some subtle form of comfort, and therefore they are not spiritual at all. They are conventional, societal activities, dressed up under a phoney title of spirituality. But actually they are part of the process of contraction.

V: It is another one of the mental tricks. I go down the "spiritual path" and I crystallize myself even more. Instead of being a soldier, now I will be a yogi or some other kind of thing. It is just another game. Most of the time that is the game I play.

Second Visitor: Could I ask an elementary question? Many teachers propose a preliminary stage in order to begin looking into oneself. They say it is beneficial to be able to focus your awareness on a particular part of your body. Some people say the abdomen, others the forehead, the top of the head, and so forth. I know this is a technique, but again from a very beginning standpoint, what are your observations on the usefulness of something like that?

RP: Ultimately, no use whatsoever. But maybe, there are people in this world whose minds have never been used properly and who miss the most elementary capacity to focus that mind on any particular problem. And it may well be that for those people who are so utterly helpless, who can't...because their attention span is so short...apply themselves to any problem, whether worldly or spiritual, it is the only way to start, to at least get some handle on their minds and create a certain quietude.

There are many people in our society who have not been properly brought up, not been educated properly, literally don't know anything about the world or themselves; and very likely what we are doing here is totally beyond them...So there are teachers, including Maharaj, who sometimes advise particular spiritual aspirants to do some simple self-observation or follow some simple techniques to that effect, like focusing their awareness on the breath. But it must be said immediately that these are absolutely preliminary stages and not everyone needs that. I think most of us are probably beyond that stage; we can go for the total picture, which is basically one of understanding—understanding what one is, in one's function, in one's relationships. I know there are people who make a big thing about awareness. I got quite a few letters to this effect. One typical comment is: "I need to read your books," or "I need to listen to your tapes, because I feel I am not proficient enough at awareness, I must be aware all the time." You must have heard similar comments. My personal view is that that kind of awareness, which is still a partial awareness, is very much an imposed practice or technique, and cannot deliver us from our ignorance. Again, I am being very personal here, I may be heretical in my view, but I feel it is much more beneficial to acquire an understanding by reading, by listening to discussions such as these, and to be reflective in a general sense, about what goes on in the world and in your life, and fully digesting it and staying with that insight. That needs a certain intensity and energy, to reflect and not have your mind go all over the place. Then this can be another kind of focusing, which I think is much more useful than focusing on the breath or on a part of your body.

Being reflective in an intensive way and going deeply into one particular area of life seems to me much more useful than practicing awareness by trying to be aware all the time. Even if that awareness succeeds, and there is that kind of attention, if it has no solid backing by understanding, is not worth a damn thing. You can be aware of every motion that goes on in this room at this moment, of your breathing, of the background noise, of my voice droning along, all these things...but it won't do very much good. What may happen, it may slow down your thought, it may quieten you a little bit. But will it give you deep insight? I doubt it. I personally view this as not the whole thing, not the whole truth, such awareness. Awareness must be within a framework of understanding and that understanding, as Maharaj keeps hammering on, comes only through a process of inquiry—systematic and deeply intensive. And that inquiry can go on in your daily activities, for example as you are doing your job, because the mind has such a capacity. It can be occupied with a routine action and at the same time it can look into itself. Has any of you experienced this? It is possible to have the mind function at different levels at the same time.

V: Oh yes, yes. But the problem with words such as "inquiry" is that they carry normally other connotations. I usually think of it as a kind of intellectual inquiry. But we are talking about something different here for which a word like inquiry does not summon up anything for me other than the kind of research you make into something scientific or artistic. We are talking here about something different. Focusing the mind somehow and practicing that...I never had much luck with it. I read about some people though who seem to have had; and if it has at least the effect of turning the mind inward to some extent, it can't be really bad in itself. As far as I am concerned, I would try anything that I thought might be somewhat useful for turning me towards what someone like Nisargadatta is talking about. There is some state in which I imagine that I am free from any impediments that keep me from being simply here in the present and not just defending, justifying, comparing—all the things that the mind normally does. I noticed Nisargadatta occasionally talks about the mantra being of some use to some. I never had any luck with that either.

RP: To *some* people he talks like that. And he also uses the word to which you object or which you think is not the absolutely correct term, "inquiry." I don't see anything wrong with it. Unless you can think of a better term?

V: No, I can't think of a better term.

RP: That is what it is, an investigation, an "examination" if you like that word better.

V: Are you using the term "inquiry" in a specific form such as Ramana Maharshi's "Who am I?"

RP: "Inquiry" is a very broad term and it can take many forms. It all comes to the same thing, whether you take it the way that Ramana Maharshi discusses it or Maharaj... Maharshi says: "Inquiry is the process of taking every outgoing thought back to its source, to its origin." Some of you may be familiar with his teachings. This is because all thoughts emanate from a primordial thought, this being the "I-thought" or "I-conceit." As we have said before, our whole way of functioning is based upon the false notion that we are independent creatures, and that is a thought, a concept. The idea of being a creature, being separate, is only in thought, a concept; it is not a reality, it is illusion. But we never inquire into that, and so it has become automatically the basic starting point for our entire thought process. Therefore, psychological thought is based upon this erroneous concept; it lies at the root of everything, of our whole world. That really is the world or space-time, is it not? I wonder if you have ever gone into this? The idea of "separateness"—this even applies on the physical level, which makes it really fascinating. In my book *Return to Meaningfulness* I have tried to inquire into this. But that is perhaps more of interest to the person who is studying cosmology. But what we are interested in here during these meetings is our psychological alienation, which is based on the same idea...

V: That is where I am right now, my general dilemma. It is probably the same with everybody else, but they may not view it the same way. I am this contracted individual through many, many years of minor accumulation of experience, which has tended to make me identified, different from you and everything...there is "I" and the other...And you are all of the "other." And I am Narcissus. And this is true of everybody. It has enormous value, that myth. We are all Narcissus, but we don't know and deny it, even the best of us, so to speak. And the problem is: How can you...I mean, I say this, but I don't really believe it...Secretly, I am above Narcissus because this is rather a horrible condition to be in, and I am gazing at myself in this damned pond for a whole life time, you see. There was a good cartoon in the *New Yorker* some time back of Narcissus sitting at the pond and Echo, his girl-friend, sitting next to him and saying: "Is there someone else, Narcissus?" [*laughter*]

Now the problem is how am I going to finally accept the fact that I am really Narcissus because if I can do that then I would really sort of explode. A transformation...I would really transcend the self, this isolated, separated self...and I would let go and quit looking into that damned pond and I would accept Echo and be part of the general thought.

Second Visitor: Why do you think that is who you are?

V: That is the observation of everybody, including myself. I tend to accept myself as everybody does...through the operations of the mind I am constantly seeking new experiences which will surpass my previous experiences and other people's experiences, and in that way I find some immunity from the suffering of the world and my own as well.

Second Visitor: But it sounds to me, as I hear you...I mean there is nothing foreign about what you are saying...what I am asking you is: Is that really who you are? You have to look at this very carefully, because I have the assumption all the time that this functioning, manifesting side of myself, which is either a nice guy or a lousy guy, or contracted, all that kind of things you are describing, all these tendencies, proclivities—narcissistic, ambitious, competitive, all this odd sort of stuff—that that is what I am and has to improve: I should regenerate, become like some other chap...I am starting with that assumption, which is the seed of the problem right there. But in this thing, this *advaita* approach, you have to really examine the basic question who the inquirer is. Is that really who you are in the first place? Or is that just an assumption? Just because everybody greets you in that way, they think that's you coming down the street. They have always seen you that way, and you take it for granted because they put out that projection that that's who you are.

The question here, this afternoon, is: Is that really me? And if it is really me, then probably it gets some sort of improvement. I have to modify something here, and I will have better relationships and I can meet these gurus, psychiatrists, do all these various exercises in concentration...all that sort of things. But what if it turns out that that is not you at all? That that is just an automatic process which has no will whatsoever, that is totally like an automaton? It just comes and goes, like a phantom in a dream...it has no meaning whatsoever. Have you ever considered that perhaps what you really are is something entirely different from all that, has even no connection with it? It is most amazing. The thing that this *advaita* is making us wonder about is this whole question, the most essential issue, of "Who am I?," as opposed to how to change myself because that is a secondary step.

RP: Which is later seen to be irrelevant.

V: All the truly enlightened ones have stated so, that we are already totally perfect; there is nothing to change.

Second Visitor: But that is not very helpful to somebody who does not see it that way. It might be equally worthwhile to look internally and see what is the make-up of the individual as he perceives himself.

V: But why is there the assumption that that is who I am? You see, all our old systems begin that way.

Second Visitor: I don't think it is useful to say I am not anything I presume that I am, because it is too frustrating to most minds.

RP: You see, it is important to look at the tool that we are using at this point, because we seem to be totally stuck here. One aspect of it is that we are using our thought to break through this static situation, to get out of this dilemma. And the very thought that we are using as a tool to break free is part of the problem: It is thought based on duality, on being a separate entity. Now can that thought, which is inherently a form of separatism, solve the problem of whether we are a separate entity or not? Obviously, it cannot. It is a cyclic process that cannot reach out beyond itself.

V: But if the thought is seeing with a mind that is not in duality, then the other will obtain.

RP: Is this a chicken-and-egg type of question? If you have seen through all this duality, you approach it entirely differently. In fact, then there is no problem.

V: If you have seen it...well, I have seen it...we have all seen it in flashes, momentarily, or perhaps for five minutes a day, or a month at a time if you are lucky. But then the major part of the time, you see the non-duality material embedded in the duality. And the question is how do you slough that off?

Second Visitor: Why do you need to slough it off?

V: Well, because...why do you need to do it?...if it is possible to do, then it is desirable to do so.

RP: Why is it desirable to do so?

V: I think it would be a return to the prior condition, which is a timeless-spaceless activity, a living in the Now, and that is a beneficent position to be in.

RP: If you have seen it properly, completely, there is no question of going back into the state of duality. Then you will see that it is not a question of non-duality being embedded in duality, but rather the other way around: duality embedded in non-duality, which leads to the total disappearance of duality in your perception. The problem, however, is that most of us have not seen it, we only think we have. It has been on the level of words, but not actually—a repetition of what somebody else has said. That is the major problem.

But even if you have understood part of this mechanism, which is an automaton, it will still manifest itself. But one need not be identified with that for one sees one is totally different, completely apart from it, something much greater, Infinite, whereas that psychosomatic entity is a very, very small thing. It always thinks small thoughts and looks for little comforts and little satisfactions. Once you have been in the other state, those little satisfactions don't satisfy any longer; so we are divorced from it. And whenever that little thing manifests itself, acts up as it were, you look at it but you are no longer it.

V: And you don't judge it.

RP: No, let it go on. In that situation, it moves and disappears. But if you still have the old assumptions, of being a separate creature, then you will see the whole world as separate beings. Whatever you look at is in duality; whatever thought one entertains is a dualistic tool, which carries the seeds of its own futility.

V: So could you say then that inquiry is really inquiry into *all* assumptions?

RP: Every assumption.

V: Because if we begin with any assumption, that makes it already impossible. It just keeps rolling along on the level of thought.

Second Visitor: What you are talking about then is the shedding of all familiarity, all assumptions. The question now is: How can we comprehend something that is incomprehensible? I believe, you can't. Some people have; that is the only sort of beacon we have to the kind of future I envision as worthwhile. Maybe it is sufficient to have faith or to surrender in general for this new condition, or "uncondition" so to speak, to arise. The thing is how this can best be perpetrated. It seems to me it has to come eventually from outside.

RP: Just wait a minute! "Outside"? It is a beautiful example how thought, dualistic in nature, tricks itself. The moment you say "outside," you have firmly established separatism, the "me" and the outside.

V: You have done as much as you can do, but it is not enough.

Second Visitor: That is just the thing: you are not supposed to *do* anything!

RP: That is a very good point, Gertrud! Marvelous.

V: I know you are not supposed to do anything, but nevertheless we are coming out on a Saturday afternoon and doing this, you see, whatever we are doing! And presumably this is going to help us, and the other people are sort of missing the boat by not being here.

RP: The way that this happens, we always want to do things and we always use that tool of thought in our doing, and we have never realized that it is possible for things to happen spontaneously without our being involved with them at all. And that is a most beautiful thing to discover! That is the beginning of true discovery. To have that mind for once get out of the habit of always probing when this probing is within narrow channels, based on assumptions. But to be in a state of inquiry...let us go into that a little. It can be a state of inquiry, without there being an "inquirer." Is that too obscure? A state of inquiry when the mind as an inquirer, a center of probing, exploring, is quiet, in abidance. Maybe then there is a state of pure intelligence. For the mind is not intelligent; it is a mechanical thing, like a computer. You program it and it will carry on its investigation, but the end result of that search is always contained in the program, in the beginning. So it never discovers anything new. It is dualistic, a linear process of thought, and our brains are the same. They are only supercomputers.

V: But how do we transcend this body-mind?

RP: Not through this process. To see that it cannot lead to a breakthrough, that is the first requirement. As long as we don't see that, your mind will come in and interfere, although it will say: I am concentrating, I am aware, I am meditating, it does all these beautiful things. But we are not breaking through that way. So let us find out if it is possible to inquire without this center of inquiry, which is the supercomputer.

V: Without any expectations.

RP: Naturally.

V: It is like, as Klein said, a listening without a listener. It is the same thing.

RP: And it is very difficult not to be carried away by the mind, with all its assumptions.

V: And to take it seriously. In a sense, when the mind is Narcissus, all of us know what that is about, how that feels, but we are taking it too seriously...

RP: You know the word "Narcissus" already implies a judgmental attitude. What is wrong with self-love? The trouble is that we don't love our self. We love that psychosomatic entity that passes for our self but which is actually like nothing, a phantom, worthless. If you love the self, you love everything, you are in a state of love. So there is nothing wrong with self-love. The point is, however, that we misunderstand what self-love is.

V: I find for instance that...well, I understand this discussion...and what you were talking about a few minutes ago...that one can concentrate on the fact that we are spirit...

RP: That is an assumption! What do you mean by "spirit"?

V: And "concentration," too? Who is the one who is doing the concentration? It is part of the mechanism.

RP: You see, we don't need any assumptions. We play with words, when we state that we are spirit, we are this and that. All that takes us away from true inquiry, because these are all words and concepts, and ultimately what *is* is not a concept. A concept is always reality narrowed down, by language, by the brain.

V: What I was trying to lead up to is that if you don't have words guided by mind, then you have to have other forms of communication. We should have to consider this in some way, and this would have to be some kind of wordless communication, such as ESP, in which everybody sitting here would be communicating without words. And this has been proved possible on the part of a handful of people throughout history.

RP: I think we are on the wrong track. We are communicating through every means at the moment, directly, verbally, electronically, on a scale that has never happened before; we have marvelous means of mass communication. But the problem is that *what* we communicate is limited. It is in itself limitation, and limitation cannot break out, for all it hears is an echo, a reflection of itself, and that reflection is of the unreal. It is based on assumptions, on what we have been told—that we are born, that we die, that we have parents, all that stuff, telling us in so many ways that we are separate beings. It has nothing in common with what *is*, which can only be found through individual inquiry, by discovering for oneself rather than listening to what somebody else has said. If one comes to these meetings and carefully listens to what other people say with the idea of picking up some information about oneself, that would be totally self-defeating. What we are trying to do here—at least I hope that we are doing this a little bit—is not to accept what somebody says; there are no authorities here. Each of us might be charged with the energy necessary to do the inquiry. Maybe then these meetings can become a center of energy that we might tap into first of all to brush away all assumptions, which is not as easy as it seems. "Assuming" is an automatic process; you live with it, it is part of you. The assumption that you are this personhood, that is the obstacle; and it is in one's blood— your blood, my blood, everyone's blood.

V: It is in every thought we have.

RP: In every thought, exactly. And so whatever you hear, if one is functioning on that basis, will be absorbed. And though people may talk about the truth of non-duality, if one is firmly in a state of duality, then that truth will be immediately corrupted. So words admittedly are inadequate, as our friend says, totally inadequate. They can only point, they cannot describe. Trying to describing the real, the indescribable, what could be more futile?

V: You can see why the mystics in any culture have adopted the means of the *via negativa*, because any attempt to approach it positively gets you into trouble.

RP: Not only that it gets you into trouble, but it is untrue. As Maharaj and others have said, you can only know what one is not. And when you have discovered that, there is no more problem in discovering what one is. But how can you put into words what one is? Who can do it? It is not possible.

V: And it is not necessary, because it is again as you said earlier an avoidance of what *is*. The preoccupation with finding, describing, changing and reaching this deep self that we have is just a movement away from staying with what *is*. Everything we do is very cunningly designed to avoid staying with exactly what *is*. Even if I put on my most sincere behavior, wishing to change because I am sort of lousy and rotten, it is still a trick, part of the movement to avoid what *is*. The hardest thing is just to rest in front of what I am, not to *do*, to make a functional effort, but just to look and observe. And if somehow it comes about, then there is some truth in the saying that the beginning is the end, there is no process. A process is always a movement in time, which is a moving away from what *is*.

Second Visitor: The only thing you can affirm then is "I am."

RP: But it is not enough just to say that. There is a world of difference between verbally uttering that truth and to be lodged in it, to *be* it. It is the same difference as between being peacefully asleep and being in one's waking state in a state of turmoil.

V: And do we see that to be in "I am" is the same as not to move away from what *is*? You may think that to be in "I am" is something fairly spiritual, mysterious, perhaps just another way of putting things, but the fact is it does not really require any preparation. Just living is the preparation.

Second Visitor: That is a good point. I think one of the things too that gets in the way in this business is that as soon as you see this as something extraordinary, you have isolated yourself from it.

V: You project in time: Maybe some day I get to that point. Then you never begin that way, you keep waiting until you get to that state.

RP: It is our natural state, but we have lost it, forgotten it.

V: It is just that we cover it up with all these other things, with all that other stuff that goes on in the mind. So if at some time we feel like Narcissus, that would be alright so long as we do not get stuck on Narcissus. Is the thing that I am stuck on today more real than what I got stuck on yesterday? None of these things proved ultimately lasting, real; they pass. You get a sense of the automatic, that there is something about this whole thing that it is on automatic pilot. It just does whatever it does, with finality. You get a sense of the absurdity of this instrument that accomplishes so much in so many ways but ultimately is so much of a dead weight. It does not deserve a whole lot of respect! [*laughter*]

Second Visitor: Also, I think there is another important aspect: it concerns not an individual action but a joint action. Your wife may yell down at you to fix something, and so you fix it. Nothing is individual, it is all a joint action, every minute. And so it is absurd to think of that little line from the giant world processor and consider modifying it.

RP: You see, trying to modify the world process is immediately our own undoing. It implies polishing, as it were, the image of what we are, the ego. But this "ego" is only an image, an imprint in one's functioning, but otherwise non-existent—in the absolute sense. Now our entire functioning is based on the kingpin of a particular "I"-image. This is really the whole process of inquiry one has to go into. So we have that assumption, although we are not conscious of it, of that kingpin, that central point, upon which all our activities rest. The obvious antidote is to become a little more aware of these superficial activities, of that center which always tries to beautify itself. In the end, someone tells you that herein lies a problem—the fact that we are narcissistic, we should not be so self-concerned and try to do something about it. But the very movement, that activity of the mind working upon the activity of self-concern, results in its actual strengthening. That is the tragedy. That is why I was so happy about what Gertrud said, that the very doing is the problem.

Can you see this clearly now? That whatever we do about our problem, it backfires. We make this into a tremendous problem, upon becoming a little aware of oneself—this ego problem, and we can't help it, we must do something about it. Immediately, automatically, mechanically, we go into action and that doing...I would go one step further, not only does the doing not help, but it strengthens the ego. Then, one must also consider this: In a deeper sense, that doing *is* the entity. Can you see that the entity is actually a process? A process of thought, of continuously interchanging images, thereby strengthening the central image which underlies all the other images about oneself.

To cut through all that "doing" might help. If we could only see the simple fact that any doing, any working upon the image of oneself, strengthens that image. As Zen Master Bankei said, it is like washing off blood with blood. It is a cyclic process, it cannot lead to anything but the status quo— the status quo being that center which does not let go of itself. There is tremendous force behind it; that center has tremendous energy, because it is the same energy that lies behind the fear of death. To wipe out that center is dying— dying to all one's notions of what we have, of what we have achieved, all these attachments, and let go of that. It is easy to say this in words but not so easy in actuality. It can only take place when the mind is totally out of the habit of doing, has finally abandoned it and is therefore completely silent. At that point, there is no doer, no inquirer, but, as we said earlier, we are that state of inquiry itself.

From the conventional point of view, in which one looks at things dualistically, this is a complete mystery. And it *is* incomprehensible. But give the incomprehensible a chance! If you don't give it a chance, if you work on the problem with your mind, analytically, discursively, or whatever, it makes it impossible for the solution to appear. But when that mind is out of the picture, when it dies to all these accumulations, layer upon layer of experience—and that is what we are as a psychosomatic entity, this process of knowledge, experience, all based upon memory—something else comes into being. If we let go of the mind even for one second and see that it is all an accumulation of artificiality—concepts and images and ideas, all carried along in memory, if one can really see that, then you are pointed at the foundation of the ego, you are hitting where it counts.

V: Right now, I am very strongly motivated to...

Second Visitor: To do what?

V: To try to be aware of this...to pay attention to my assumptions, and so forth, but here I am *doing* it again.

RP: Another person, another human being, can only be a catalyst. As soon as you take his words as a method, a prescription, you are lost.

V: You have to kick him out, too.

RP: Otherwise, you throw the responsibility, yours, upon someone else; you abandon your own responsibility. This is a work without working, one might say...it is very subtle.

V: I think a time comes when you have no choice. Then all you can do is look. It is not a question of being stirred up...

RP: Being stirred up or motivated, that is a kind of encouragement...then that again is the old thought!

V: You just have no choice. There you are, there is only you to look at it...and the book is spread out in front of you...Of course, anything you do is "you." Anything that is happening at the moment is your actuality. I am not saying your real self, because that is an assumption. It may not be your real self, but the process is going on, whatever it is. And it is there in front of you. It does not take an inch of effort at all. That is the first thing to realize. Everyone else is giving you a prescription for all kinds of effort...if I can only be a little more intensive in my meditation, all that sort of things...it is so much evasion, all that, and maybe some people, as Robert said, have to go through that kind of song and dance...it is here, it is this very second, this Now, there is no other time to see what it is. There is no mystery...we make a mystery out of this thing, we think it is something only very special chaps can get the hang of...It is not like that at all. It is exactly what *is*, flowing along with it. And seeing that, the mind feels funny in that position. It says: I rather work on something else...make myself into something half-way decent...all that we try to do, just to escape from this actual moment, the Now. And it really does not take any effort at all, it is just there. It is only the notion we have that it takes effort, that it takes a tremendous grasp. But it is all there, it is just like reading a newspaper.

RP: And the notion that some persons are more gifted or qualified than others is equally erroneous. Because there are no persons in the first place! It is the general ignorance that we are tackling, you tackle your ignorance, and I tackle mine—the general ignorance that we have imbibed. We are brought up with this Ignorance, and it is not just an individual ignorance. It has gone into our minds, but we have not invented it, we are not the creators of it.

V: Are you talking about socialization?

RP: Yes, perhaps a better word would be "culturalization," the insertion into our minds of all kinds of worldly knowledge and concepts, including religious indoctrination. All that has to be given up before a total transformation is possible. There are those who think they simply cannot let go of all this worldliness; they quote a lack of spiritual inclination or giftedness as an excuse. Their attitude is: "Let me forget it, and leave me just to be worldly and carry on in my ignorance." That is O.K. too, if one can be so absolutely honest and consistent. But then one must also watch out for another kind of trap, the duality of being worldly and not wanting to give up one's worldly activities, on the one hand, and on the other hand still striving to delve into these unworldly things and think that one is going somewhere spiritually as well. You can't have your cake and eat it. At some point, a decision will have to be made, based on the question: "Am I going to start from no assumptions, with a blank slate, which means immunizing myself against all external influences through properly digesting, understanding them—even my own past experience, all based upon arbitrary, and therefore false assumptions—or do I feel more secure and happy as an ordinary worldly human being?" That is up to each of us, and the decision will have to be a spontaneous one.

V: Because if I stay with one assumption, I have bought into the whole package—they are all the same. One assumption is like another. One image is like another, one concept is like another; they are all on the same level. So, as Robert said, at a certain stage I have to see the whole thing I have been entertaining all these years as a fraud, that I have to discard it entirely in order just to stay with what *is*. And I don't do that with a will, by effort; it just comes about spontaneously. It really comes about naturally from seeing how everything is completely automatic and non-individualistic.

RP: First one must see that one is confused and how confused one is, and recognize the source of all that confusion. And then one asks oneself: What is it that makes me tick? Is it the truth, or is it following the rules and laws of society, flowing along with the whole tenor of society by accepting all the ideals and concepts we are bombarded with?

So I am leaving you with an enormous area for quiet observation and contemplation, to digest all that—a goodly slice of homework.

This must be the conclusion of our session for this Saturday.

10.

SELF-INQUIRY

Robert Powell: Let us continue tying up any loose bits, any unfinished business from our previous meetings. That is really what we are doing at every one of these meetings. Unlike acquiring knowledge on the physical level—knowledge of the world, which is cumulative, where we need to extend our knowledge gradually, bit by bit, until we have the total picture when we can say: "Yes, I am competent, I know the subject"—what we are doing here can never be cumulative, because the kind of knowledge we want to have, which is called *jnana*, is not to be obtained as the result of integrating a lot of data, bits of knowledge. If one thinks one can acquire more and more knowledge at each of these meetings until the day that you know it all, then you will be doing this for the rest of your days.

In this area, if one goes into one particular aspect of one's life so deeply that one goes beyond all the knowledge acquired from hearsay, all second-hand knowledge, if one really penetrates that deeply into one particular aspect of one's being, then that is enough. But most of us find this very difficult. Somehow we are impatient, we think we have gone deeply enough into one particular aspect of our lives, and we want to jump onto something else. In this fashion we ever go leapfrogging, and so always stay within the field of the known, which is the field of experience. But that way does not lead to the Unknown, because the Unknown is at once very close to where we are and at the same time, it is beyond all that—beyond the process of learning in the conventional way, memorizing, practicing, trying out new techniques. The Unknown is totally beyond all these things.

It sometimes happens to a human being quite spontaneously that he finds himself with a deep insight into the nature of reality, without having made any effort whatsoever, without apparent cause. That experience of finding without trying to find, of discovering without working towards such discovery, is rather miraculous. It has been called "seeing into the Emptiness," or "realizing the Emptiness." And others who have never had this insight will start building upon the word "Emptiness," giving it all kinds of meanings. They might think it is a kind of destruction, annihilation. After all, the word itself has certain negative connotations, but there is no way that you can define what that insight is. The "Emptiness" is merely a code word for a different state of consciousness. Perhaps one might say, it is a state of total otherness that has to be discovered.

One understands that the world that exists in actuality is totally other than the world existing in our thought. The picture of the world that we always carry with us is essentially what we have acquired from hearsay, but we have lived with it for so long that it has become second nature to us. We have swallowed it—this ideation of what the world is like or should be like—and that is the only world we know, the only life we know. So if one has such an experience of an insight— I must be careful here, it is not actually an "experience," it is a sudden change of focus, a shift in one's seeing—if one is in that state, then one has no words to talk about it and convey it to another. All one can say is: the conventional world, the world of concepts about what *is* is totally false. And the real is totally other than that familiar world in which the word "emptiness" has a commonly accepted connotation. But the

Emptiness I am referring to is at once everything, it contains the totality of our existence, the "me" as well as the "non-me," and therefore it is a state of fulness.

As I said, there are people who have come to this spontaneously without asking for it—it just happened. Others have come to it through a lengthy process of investigation, inquiry. Some have done this on their own, others needed the presence, the guidance, of a spiritual teacher or guru. And there is nothing in the world that can be done to determine when or how one will have such an insight. If you use your mind, your thought process, to try to grasp it, it will ever elude you for the simple reason that the mind that is always active, is itself the hindrance, the stumbling block, the barrier to knowing, to finding oneself with what *is*. And it is the *only* barrier. Now the mind can trick itself and say: I am not really there, I am in a state of abeyance, I am quiet, I am silent. But it is still the mind that says it. If there is a real subsidence of that mind activity, there is nothing being said because there is no one to say it.

There is a total silence, the silence that comes not only from within the mind but also from without. That does not mean that you go out of your mind, or that you can't use knowledge any longer. But you use your mind only as a tool whenever applicable. It is the first time you can use your mind in a sane way, for the very reason that it is merely a tool. It is purely a means of functioning on the physical level, and there is no longer any psychological interference. After all, the mind is a psychological disturbance when used outside its proper field of operation. It is based on a total misconception of what we are. Mind as consciousness has no form, no structure. It is nothingness—a nothingness that contains everything. But at some point, thought through identification has become an entity, it has created that entity, the "you," the "me." And once it has happened, that "me" will continue to aggrandize itself, build itself up, give itself security as that entity. This whole process is based on a misunderstanding. Thought through memory has built up a speck of consciousness as a solid entity, and henceforth a whole life is lived from that point of view, through that entity that has self-created boundaries and limits.

We have alienated ourselves from the Emptiness which is the real and which is beyond space and time, and therefore has no limits. Because of that, our daily life is an eternal struggle to *be*, to *become*—it is a process of resistance. And on that level, there obviously cannot be any way out. Because one never investigates how this whole process has come into being, the very mind that wants to break out and find deliverance must go into itself and see how it has come into being, how it was born. And even when it probes the ordinary state of mind and how to get out of the prison of the self, it uses tools which are totally inappropriate for the inquiry. Can we see that?

The tools of the mind are essentially time-bound. And when the mind wants to break out and it projects a reality which lies beyond, that "reality" is still the mind caught in space and time. So one really has to look within oneself. If one thinks that one can investigate, can start this process of inquiry with our normal state of consciousness, then it is a circular process that cannot lead to anything new, to any breakthrough. The entity that has been established in space and time will only function through space-time. It will try to achieve, satisfy its desires which are all time-based, goal-oriented, and it will compare, which is the activity within space because the effort to *be* entails comparison. One wishes to *be* or to *become* on the basis of what others are. So time and space, once set into motion through the creation of the "me," will ever continue in this expansive mode. Then even spirituality becomes a mere modification of the worldly life, of that "me" doing more of the same thing that it has been doing all along.

If one has seen clearly how the center comes into being, that at present one has one's abode in space and time and that whatever one does in that abode can only be a continuation of the old process, then one must conclude that only when one's abode lies beyond space-time can there be a different way of life. Which is really only another way of saying that the psychosomatic entity with which we live, that we think is us, is not the place to be. It is an object that appears in consciousness and is to be observed, *only* to be observed, to be witnessed, but not to be identified with. And many people have a difficulty at this point; they will say: "Yes, I have been told by my guru that I am not really that psychosomatic entity, so I must ignore it, but I feel I can't and that is my problem." How does one get out of this quandary?

The easiest and surest way is if you can see for yourself how that psychosomatic entity has come into being, and you can perceive its unreality. You can see that it is not an absolute and has come about through a complicated but arbitrary process of thought, and ultimately is only a concept, an image. It has no individuality. If you can naught it in that manner, then this is the first step—and it may also be the last. For that you must be able to look at it, what goes on inside the mind, the mind and the body as a psychosomatic entity. You must look just as you look at nature—the ocean, the mountains, etc. Normally we don't look like that. We look *through* this psychosomatic entity, which gives us a very limited view and one in which everything is colored by the entity's essential characteristics. Whatever we look at is from a background, based on memory, conditioning. So if one can really detach oneself from all that knowledge, all these ideations that we have about the body and the mind, that first step may already be a liberation.

If you can't do that, you have to pursue your inquiry further. If you can't see clearly, right away, that that psychosomatic entity is false, is a fraud, then you have to stay with it. Then, for example, you have to look at all your motives, and see if there is not a psychological component in your relationships. You will surely discover how every action is driven by the psychosomatic entity. This goes for action in all our relationships, those with humans as well as with ideas, and with the cosmos.

From where does our ultimate motive for action spring? Upon examination, one will see it always comes from the energy that keeps the psychosomatic entity intact, which is the energy of the ego. That inquiry is really one's spiritual practice, if one wants to use that term, or *sadhana*. Ever stay with that.

If you are not fortunate enough to have that insight into the Emptiness spontaneously, then one should be in a continual state of inquiry. And the purpose of these meetings is just that, to form a part of one's *sadhana*. I say "part," because it does no good to inquire only while we are sitting here. Maybe the mind is a little quiet, and maybe you feel a little lighter than usual, somewhat unburdened, but the moment you walk out of here all your problems are rushing back and one has lost that flame of attention or awareness. It is gone. It happens to all of us. Before you can say anything the mind is working overtime; it is working furiously on one problem after another. In other words, it is caught once again within space-time. Always struggling to achieve, to maintain itself. And in that state there is no freedom, obviously. Freedom to be real, not to be an entity which is a very, very small thing. And that practice is not a technique in the usual sense, because you do not use any knowledge, you do not use any methods, any formulas, but it is a staying with the inquiry. At the same time one maintains a certain level of aloofness, like ideally the scientist is in his laboratory, observing, without being in the least emotionally wrapped up in his findings. One has to be like a bulldog, obstinate, although the world is full of distractions, amusements, escapes. You must stay with it. You mustn't say: "I will do it tomorrow; I will look into it, or next week or next month, next year." Then you miss. You must have the energy not to let go.

V: Excuse me, Robert. What are you not letting go of? What are you being obstinate over?

RP: I will tell you, I will explain it. It is almost like a negative process. Because if you say to yourself, "I want to unite myself with the real," that "real" in one's present state of consciousness can only be a projection. For the mind can't reach it, cannot touch the real.

V: Is there anything in the present that is the real, that gives some taste of that?

RP: It is always there, the real, but we are estranged from it. However, it is available at any moment. We are alienated from it only by the mind. The mind is the obstacle, the screen, the barrier, as it were. So when I use that word "obstinacy," it implies a certain energy, a certain intentionality, a longing if you like, at the back of your worldly activities, that is focused on not forgetting that we live in delusion. We live from a false point of view. We live as separate entities, which have been brought about by a misunderstanding, by thought. It is not that you or me have created that entity; there is no entity, there is no "you" and "me." It is an optical illusion, as it were. But what one *is*, is nothing, it is a state of nothingness.

So one must be serious, one must be earnest about the real. First of all, see that what we do now is engage in a kind of self-deception, that all our actions, all our thought processes, are based on the misunderstanding that one is some thing, some entity—which is the root cause of the illusion. And it needs a lot of honesty, and humility, because in our normal state of consciousness there is always lurking in the back of the mind, as its engine, the "I"-conceit. I call it that because there is not merely a picture of the "I," but one that has built into it a conceit, a vanity, because if it were really an image only, like the image produced on a photographic film, there would be no process of psychological corruption. Then you would just see yourself as a mere functional entity.

But that is not the world we live in. That psychological island wishes to expand; it is always comparing itself with others who have the same mode of seeing. And so we live in this insane world, always in conflict with our fellow-beings primarily because thought has produced the illusion of the entity, the "I," and from and through that the whole world is built up. And unless you can undo that, nothing will be of any avail. And that is our "work"; in a sense it is a sacred task. You really have to see it, even for one short moment, that this thing that has come into being is totally unreal. Then to be obstinate means not to be satisfied with it, never let it get the upper hand, even though you may lose your awareness temporarily; then the first step back to full awareness is to be attentive of one's own inattentiveness. And being aware of that inattentiveness comes with observing one's relationships, one's motivations. That is the only way.

As I said earlier, we are doing this, practicing this kind of meditation, in meeting after meeting while tying up any loose bits, any unfinished business. And we will go on doing this. It is right that we do it, but we haven't got the expectation—or I have not got the expectation, I don't know about you—of eventually having a complete picture, having tied up all the loose ends and then "having arrived." Paradoxically, in the process of tying up loose bits, the moment may arrive that in looking at one particular fragment—but looking with such intensity, clarity and in such great depth—you don't have to go on inquiring any further about any other aspect of your life. The aspect under scrutiny is sufficient, it will give its clues, the solution to everything. It is as it were, hologrammatic. That small part of life that one is looking at so intensely, so deeply, contains within itself the whole. It is not like a jigsaw puzzle where you have to put together all the pieces of your life. Just look at one piece and the puzzle starts fitting together by itself.

V: And what is that piece, Robert? What is the piece that you look at?

RP: It could be any piece. As I said, any of our "loose bits." It is not the content that matters, but the going beyond, the transcendence, that leads directly to the touchstone. In fact, it is the very contentlessness that is the touchstone.

V: The reason I ask is that in reading all sorts of literature on mysticism after twenty years or so one big problem I saw in a lot of it is that much of what was there led you away from this. You focused on other concepts, things that led you astray. The value I saw in something like Nisargadatta's version—he is not the only one but one of the few that I read that said there is something right now in the immediate here and now, some touchstone that you have already that you can work with—is where he states it is the sense of your being.

RP: It is also called "beingness" or "knowingness."

V: The sense of being itself. So in a sense you have the ability at any second to discriminate between what is going to take you deeper into the now and what is going to lead you away, and it is this beingness. As soon as you are taken away from that sense of beingness, you know the direction is faulty. Wherever you are going has not got anything to do with what we are seeking. Because once you lose the sense of beingness, you are off on some other trip. So the value I saw is in having some touchstone that when you got lost among your thoughts and what not, you have always got that. And it seems to me that Nisargadatta talks about shortening the intervals when you have no sense of your beingness.

RP: The more you can be attentive, the more you can be aware of your thought—with its deep-rooted habits, illusions, misunderstandings—the more you can do that, the shorter the intervals will be of your inattentiveness. And that inattentiveness is when you function exclusively on the level of space and time. Whenever you are in the abode of space-time, you will be the slave of thought. Only when you are in the abode beyond space-time, you will not be subject to any limitations. I don't know whether any of you has ever had an experience of that, the state of Emptiness. Paradoxically, one might say subjectively there is a feeling of being surrounded by, or floating in, immense space although you are not in space-time. Space-time does not exist anymore. But even to say that one is "surrounded" is misleading, as is "floating," since it implies "weight," because like the very basis of our language, these expressions are spatial constructs. There is only this great emptiness, this spaciousness, and one is the witness, a mere witness to the functioning of one's own body as well as other bodies. That is the nearest I can come to express it.

V: But in that state, whatever else it may be, there is the suspension of that activity in consciousness, the content of consciousness...There is no content of that consciousness, is there?

RP: It is not that greatly different, but there is a functioning that goes on without you doing anything about it. You are merely looking at it..

V: It might slow it down. It does have a tendency as such...At present, the manifestation is very neurotic and agitated, and there is no question...in fact, it might even temporarily suspend itself entirely. For a moment, it could happen.

RP: It isn't there. There is no psychological activity of any kind whatsoever. And then you know what one is doing in the other state of consciousness.

V: The need for this touchstone became apparent to me several years back; it is just a single sense and it contains certain kinds of touchstone words: "Be conscious as the feeling of being and realize that it is radiant happiness or freedom itself."

RP: I don't know whether those words even touch it...They are just words.

V: Well, on the contrary. I find them to be much preferable to the traditional emphasis on emptiness.

RP: Why do you want a description?

V: Well, emptiness is a description of a vacuum.

RP: I was just saying, in no way it is that: it is a mere code word. It cannot tell you while in the state of consciousness, of being within space-time...it cannot tell you anything about it. It is really an "otherness" and therefore incapable of being defined in known terms. Maharaj calls it a "non-state."

V: Radiant happiness is just the very thing.

RP: But when you say "radiant happiness" you will immediately interpret it according to your concepts of happiness and radiance which are conventional.

V: Not necessarily.

RP: That is all you know. It is like telling a blind man what color is. It can't be done. But it is not necessary anyway.

V: It is dangerous to even look for a touchstone. The mind wants to do that, there is no question about it, because we want to hold on to something...so I won't get lost in all these

thoughts, and stuff like that. The problem is the thing that
sets off that whole process of wanting to hold on to it is the
very thing that you should want to get away from! It is kind
of a paradox. The thing that we are trying to find freedom
with is the very obstacle to freedom, disguised in another
kind of way.

RP: The seeker is the sought!

V: Everything I do really is an appearance in consciousness,
including my wish to be free...the whole thing...So is it possible for there to be something entirely without any character-
istic at all, beyond any name, beyond any shape or any help,
which is totally unconditioned, obviously, and which can see
all this?

RP: You know this raises some interesting, much wider,
issues. Even in one's description of the physical world, if you
go down to the very limits of knowledge, as physicists are
presently doing in their investigation of the so-called "fundamental particles," they find it totally impossible to pin down
those particles within any conventional frame of reference,
any traditional terminology, or grasp them through pure intuition.

Now if one reflects on this for a moment, one will see
that it must necessarily be so, because it is a departure from
the world of space-time to penetrate to the very rock bottom
of what is on the material level. One *must* come upon a great
puzzle, because all our familiar yardsticks and touchstones,
on the coarsest level of experiencing, which is seeing, touch-
ing, smelling—the sensory impressions that we get on the
macro level—don't exist any longer. Because those attributes
are part of the perceiver. It is one process. It is not that there
are the properties of matter on the one hand, and there is the
perceiver on the other hand. It is one continuum, an interchange of sensory perceptions, and that in itself means that

the thing that I am looking at is in a way an extension of my own apparatus. It is a circular process, like rewording knowledge about oneself, one's own little world, in endless ways, but never reaching out to the new, the unknown. That is why the approach to self-inquiry through science is a dead end.

V: When you are conscious of the feeling of being and realize it is radiant happiness or freedom itself, what more do you want?

RP: You personally may have had that insight, but the question is to convey it to me, who still lives exclusively in the world of space-time, who has never had any such insight, and has always accepted everything from hearsay about the world. How would you possibly convey anything of this deeper reality to me who has lived all his life in illusion? It can't be done. I would not be able to come anywhere near tasting that perfume of the real, if I have not already developed a bit of its taste within myself.

V: In Nisargadatta, don't you have the feeling that he is constantly referring back to the sense of "I am"? Now, when we talk of a touchstone—maybe that isn't the best term to use—but isn't it something like the sense of "I am", the immediacy of being oneself?

Second Visitor: You are already that, you know. The way one is putting it is very critical. Because if I get the notion that I want to get into it, the "I am," as though I am out of it, then I am already setting up a dichotomy. So in a way the whole thing is false from the start, any move I make in that direction. What else could I be but the "I am"—all the time?

V: No, I am not trying to be it, it is more in the nature of a reminder that that's what you are. Because most of the time, the mind is doing something else, does it not? It is occupied with various sorts of ideas and activities. But instantaneously, at any moment, we can have a sense of what we are. Is not that what Maharaj is saying? He is constantly reminding you there is a special value in bringing yourself back to the sense of "I am," and there is a method of sorts in his non-method, it seems to me. And that is in bringing you back to that. I am not putting it very well but that seems to be what he is about.

I am not sure that even a lot of the other teachers are not doing the same. Some of them talk about it—it is true we can't use this as a general example—these koans and mantras and that sort of thing. I think even the people who use these or have used them traditionally have the notion that they are not anything in themselves. They are a tool only to take you so far, and then you must throw the tool away and go on from there.

Second Visitor: Well, I think Nisargadatta says you have to go beyond this "I am" and throw out even the use of that as something you might grasp as a touchstone.

V: But not necessarily in the preliminary stages. I was reading a bit of Saint John of the Cross the other night and he is talking about how in the early stages he was advising people that in meditation—and he distinguished meditation from contemplation by saying that meditation always has some kind of object—they should meditate on some object. It could be Jesus, prayer, it may also be something like this gentleman mentioned...in the East I suppose it would be a mantra or something like that. And at some point along the way, the inadequacy of that becomes manifest to you and then you move on to some other stage...he talks about "contemplation" in which there is no object and into which one naturally evolves through the use of more meditative types of techniques, as he describes them. So I would think with Nisargadatta you have some sort of object...but that is not the end in itself but maybe the gateway through which you have to pass.

RP: But isn't there a danger in all this when you talk about a gateway and touchstone that one has the underlying assumption that somehow we can control this, we can do something, we can reach towards it, and that it is strictly progressive?

V: Well, don't you believe it is possible to realize something in this life?

RP: But how? Not through doing, not through working towards it. Because who is doing the working towards it, who is groping towards it? You see, we come back to the old truth which we have been repeating here all along, that first one must find out what that entity is which is doing all this, that is saying I must have a touchstone, I must hold on to the "I am" state...The entity is the product of a mistaken identity. There is no entity.

V: And there's nothing to be done then.

RP: Therefore that process can never reach the other, because the other is already here. When the false identity is seen as false, then it happens by itself. Then there is a spontaneous process or rather, event.

V: But even when the entity is there...it is there, it could never not be there.

RP: Of course, as an appearance. That very appearance seen through for what it is in its real nature, is the real; and there is only the real.

V: These notions, superimposed, about being caught and wanting to get out...it is all a marvelous game the mind plays with itself, creating a notion of the prison, the notion of the self, having to get out of the prison; and it continually perpetuates it, because I must do something to get out...If I am there, I have to get out. The whole thing is a trick and a delusion.

RP: So what do we arrive at, what can we do?

V: Nothing.

RP: We can *see* only. The most efficacious way is not do anything about it, but only to see that we are nothing, which is a tremendous letting go. Because it means that you are out of this whole, comparative social process of struggling to be, to become. When you see that you are nothing, that the whole thing has come about as a mirage, as a misperception, there is nothing to be done. The real manifests at that moment. But only when you see it, not before.

V: But the thing is to understand the real and then to transcend it and go on to something else. And eventually you have realized the reality.

RP: No, no. That is a completely old and erroneous way of looking at things, that is the thinking mechanism putting something into different words, which it is always doing. Transcending means to go beyond; but there is no need to go beyond at this point, because you are already there. You are already the real, the perfect, and there is nowhere further to go on to. There is the idea of perfection, which is essentially a societal thing. The world tells you, you must better yourself, you must become perfect—all the religions are saying that. But it is essentially a worldly idea, based on the idea that you are something that needs to be polished, to be beautified. But you are beautiful right now, but you don't know it!

V: You must realize your own beauty, without the entity playing to it. The entity is nothing but a contraction from the real.

RP: I think we should get away from this word "contraction." It is a very useful term but only on the psychological level, not the spiritual. Contraction happens once you are established as an entity with a particular identity, when you feel threatened by others, by other entities, and you want to safeguard, you want to build up the security of, that entity and strengthen your own identity in the process. The contraction then takes place as a sort of bracing yourself against the peril that might lie in wait for you out there.

V: All the time!

RP: All the time.

V: It is an activity.

RP: And therefore you say, I must transcend and do this and that. But it is based upon a misapprehension. It will therefore never lead to the real...

V: The mind comes in belatedly, historically, in the development of the individual and the race. But the contraction begins with birth, the crisis of birth and the pain and whatever other things...The pain does not come around for some while. So when the mind comes in, it only comes in to serve those instincts and to aggrandize the individual in the complexities of life. So it is a feeling business, a feeling that...

RP: We were talking about the word "contraction" and I had not quite finished with it. Contraction is when that entity has crystallized. It expands and contracts as a way of dealing with its environment. But when it is seen that there is no entity, that one is nothing, you can no longer talk about contraction. Because nothingness, nothing, cannot contract. It is only when you have a center that it can expand and contract. But when the center is seen to be void, it voids all those

notions. Those notions have fallen away. When that nothingness remains, it is no longer possible to contract or to
expand, because contraction and expansion are processes in
space and time. So when one has one's abode in the spaceless
and timeless, there is no contraction, there is nothing that
can contract—one is All. And the All is the Nothing, or the
Nothing is the All.

V: Robert, when you are describing the entity which we are,
which is built up...I think you said that it has no individuality. But isn't that kind of a paradox? We want to have no "I,"
or no ego, so if it already has this "no-individuality," the entity has achieved part of what you are talking about—the sup-
pression of the ego, its banishment into the cosmic unity.

RP: Nobody really wants to do away with identity, nobody.
Because that is like dying.

V: But you said the entity has no individuality.

RP: That's right, not actually, inherently. It has only apparent
individuality. It is thought that has created that false ideation
of identity. And that is the only way, the correct way, to perceive this. There is nothing to destroy, you see. You cannot
destroy the identity or the entity, because who is doing the
destroying? It is that same entity! Therefore it is deceiving
itself; it will not do it, regardless of how much lip-service it
pays to its own destruction. Just like a dog chasing after its
own tail—it will never succeed. It simply cannot be this way.

It can only happen by itself, without cause; and that happens when one perceives one's own nothingness. Because
what is there that you can call your own? Is there anything
that qualifies? Not even your thought is your own! There is
only thought. Your body...is your body your own? Is there a
body that is born and dies, or is that something we picked up
from information, from the society, from our parents? All

these are entities within space-time with which we are identified. And if all that is gone, then you are out of it. Then you have your abode in the spaceless and timeless. And nothing can touch you, threaten you anymore. There is no question of contracting or expanding, because you are what *is*, you are the All.

V: But he is confused on this question...

Second Visitor: Are you using the word identity and individuality as the same thing...?

RP: Essentially, they are the same.

But it is your job, our job, to ever inquire, penetrate into the illusion of being something and discovering that nothingness. That is the *sadhana*, that is our work, the spiritual practice; it is not a repeating of something or going through a technique and applying it. It is ever inquiring at every serious moment of reflection: What am I? That is what it boils down to. And to see that one is nothing, that all that one is is a build-up, an accretion, an accumulation of concepts, of images. That even this body is not mine, is not yours. The mind has said it is mine, the mind which itself is unreal, which is only a set of concepts, built upon such flimsy things as memory. Without that flimsy thing, there is nothing...

V: I understand my body is not "mine" because that to which you are referring does not possess that body...It implies that you are referring to some individuality.

RP: Correct. Normally we are identified with that form. I am talking about our false image as having that body. But when you investigate, is there such a thing as a body? And is that body "mine"? You will come to a different understanding. There is nothing that has any permanent property or quality attached to it; everything is transitory. Everything is moving, and nothing has self-nature.

V: So if it can be conceived, sensed or in any way designated as something concrete, it is not of the real; hence the expression *neti-neti*, not this, not this...

RP: Everything is changing—changeable and changing; and has to, in order to have this world of everlasting change there has to be a stable background, a Source, of unchangingness, of the unchanging. Otherwise, we would not be able to be aware of "change" in the first place, just like wetness can only be detected by something dry and light is only detected when one knows darkness.[1]

That source of the unchanging, of the changeless, must be beyond space and time. For as long as it is within space-time, there is change; there will be birth and there will be death.

V: I see that, but I don't see that there must be something that does not change and is permanent.

RP: You have to see that intuitively.

V: It seems just as valid to suppose that everything could be changing as that there has to be something that does not change.

---

1 *Note to the reader:* Throughout Indian spirituality the tenet prevails that only the Unchanging is real. This usually unspoken assumption was one of the fundamental differences between the world views of J. Krishnamurti, for whom everything was transient, and that of *Advaita Vedanta*. How can its truth be shown? I see the changeable as that which appears to exist for an infinitesimally short period of time, but is immediately transformed into something other than itself. Since it is continually in the process of disappearing (and reappearing as other than itself, and then disappearing again as such), how can it be said to be the real? The Unchanging alone is that against which all change is to be measured. This can be intuitively understood in a simple manner by analogy with the following experience common to all: Only from a stationary railway coach can the movement or lack of movement of other carriages be ascertained with certainty.

RP: That is the You, that is the Self, that one really *is*, timelessly.

V: What is it that witnesses all these changing objects? Is that something that changes?

SV: I think I am changing.

V: Yes, but is that what is really witnessing, or are you referring to the mind which keeps changing all the time?

SV: The mind.

RP: You are watching with your mind?

V: I don't know of anything else within me. I don't see anything else.

RP: You cannot see it, because whatever you see is not you. The eye sees but cannot see itself! We have gone through this before.

V: I know, that is a vicious circle.

RP: No, no. You can only know what you are not. And only when you have fully seen what one is not, totally seen it, and there are no questions left, then only you know what *is*, but it is not an ordinary knowing in the intellectual sense. Then you *are* that.

V: There is one more point. Everything you see now, everything that is seen, is an appearance in consciousness, in awareness; it all appears within awareness, in no other place. The same awareness is there before you were born; when you were a little child; now; when you are going to be old and your teeth drop out...all of that, that awareness never changes. The things that are seen change. The ideas you have about yourself change; objects change, everything else is changing, but awareness itself is the one thing that doesn't. This is what we are talking about, this "I am" sense. However, you don't have to find this, you don't have to look, you don't have to catch it, or anything like that. And even if you caught it, it would not have any characteristics, because everything appears within this. This is our Source, our base, and it never changes. It can't change. But because the mind is very confused, has this case of mistaken identity, I identify with the body apparatus as being my actual self. And that is the confusion of the mind. It is no problem for us, what we are in our real nature. It is only a mental problem.

RP: Everything changes, is in a flux; only the Ultimate Seer does not change. He is the Ultimate Background, the background to all other backgrounds.

V: Well, I am not aware of knowing or seeing anything before I had a mind. And I suspect that after I die I will also not see and be aware of anything. So there is another problem there.

Second Visitor: For the moment, we can forget about before you were born. But throughout your life, my life, everything appears in consciousness, all the time. It is the one quality, relatively stable quality, that we have throughout our whole life. It is the only thing we can count on. I keep posing: once I believe I am a schoolboy, another time I think I am getting married, another of being a romantic lover, another time I have an idea that I am desperate—all these various poses go on through me but all are experiences in awareness.

RP: Not only that, but the moment one says "after I die," "before I was born," it is still based on the fallacy of the entity, when space-time is no longer there. Space-time does not really exist! You are not limited, you have no limitations either in space or in time. You have your abode in the beyond, which is here at every moment. And then, it is not you who is born and who dies. Maybe the body is born and dies. But that body is born, actually, any moment the mind becomes active. Intermittently, the body is born. Some of us may remember that Jean Klein said essentially the same thing, when he was talking in this house. Do you remember that?

We create that body; that body is not actually there, it only comes into being through the mind. When the mind starts moving, the body comes into being—not only your own body but all bodies in the world. In fact, the whole world comes into being through that mind. It is not the other way as we think, that the mind and the body are within the world. The world is created by mind activity. Only through the mind activity is there a world. That is an essential truth to grasp.

V: This is an important distinction, because your statement is from a purely empirical standpoint, from the standpoint of what you can know.

RP: Yes.

V: It seems to me it has to be so. Because the only means we have of knowing the world is...

RP: Through consciousness.

V: Is through consciousness. Empirically this is so. This is how the world is re-created every time.

RP: You can only know it through consciousness; that is therefore the primary reality. And whatever you perceive is not only *in* consciousness, it is also *of* consciousness; it cannot be anything but that. The whole world hangs by this very slender thread of consciousness. No consciousness, no world.

V: My mind's interpretation, or what my mind can do with the sensory input...I am doing this backward. The world is to me what my senses create in my mind, and I suspect it is very similar in me and you, but the world itself does not depend on me. If I go, it will still be there...This process is structuring something in my mind, at least my interpretation...

Second Visitor: But your idea of "you" and "me" is already ...[*unintelligible*]

RP: There must be a perceiver for that world to be, always. They both represent one continuum. Suppose there were no sentience left at all, there would be no world. For whom could that world appear? Don't you see that the perceiver and the world are one? There would only be the Unmanifest, the Infinite Potentiality for the creation of the manifest—the Absolute, which is even now.

Excuse me, I don't mean to be rude, but you go on talking in a circular manner. All your thinking is based upon "I am this entity, I am this body."

V: Right.

RP: And that is what we have disputed in the first place. So one can go on arguing about this until Doomsday. Until one knows what the perceiver is, the person who is perceiving and who is thinking about this...The thinker must understand his own process of thinking and see how it is based on certain assumptions, which he goes on repeating endlessly in the process of investigating, and then to see so thoroughly that that process of investigation based upon being an entity in space and time will always be self-enclosed, always repeating its own premises and assumptions and therefore never really comprehend what lies at the root of all this. It can't do anything else.

V: That is the way it looks, there is no other way.

RP: That means an awakening. To wake up and see that this whole world, this whole life of ours, is a dream, from which we need to wake up, urgently. Unless one has gone into this and woken up as to what the thinker is, we cannot tackle any problem, radically, in such manner that you don't have to go on ever looking at and studying new aspects of our existence in an accumulative way. As we started this meeting, we were saying if we could get to the bottom of one aspect of our life, who is the one who is observing it, and totally understand him, and see the falsity of our conventional ideas about the observer and discover that the observer in actuality does not exist, is totally nothing, then with that view of nothingness, with that living truth of being nothing, there is a transformation and all these questions fall away. They are seen to be false questions, false probings, not the real investigation.

INSPIRING BOOKS
FROM BLUE DOVE PRESS

The Ultimate Medicine
by Sri Nisargadatta Maharaj, edited by Robert Powell
ISBN: 1-884997-09-0   240pp $14

"In *The Ultimate Medicine*, Nisargadatta, like the great sages of old India, elucidates the nature of Ultimate Reality clearly and simply. He makes the highest Self-realization a matter of common understanding so that any sincere seeker can grasp the essence of it."

—David Frawley, O.M.D., author of *Ayurvedic Healing*

The Experience of Nothingness
by Sri Nisargadatta Maharaj, edited by Robert Powell
ISBN 1-884997-14-7   185 pages $14

The depth and subtlety of the treatment of the subject make these dialogues virtually unsurpassed in the spiritual literature. In this volume Maharaj for the first time reveals the rationale for his apparently brusque manner with certain visitors, not allowing them to stay for an extended period. Maharaj also explains why he rarely agrees with his visitors, even when they seem to make a valid statement or give a correct answer to his question.

An exposition of the ancient teaching of non-duality or *Advaita* at its best.

Collision with the Infinite
by Suzanne Segal
ISBN: 1-884997-27-9 (Available August 1996)   Price to be announced

The autobiography of an American sage.

"To anyone interested in the subject [*Advaita*], I would say read this book."   —Ramesh Balsekar, author of *Consciousness Speaks*

"This is an extraordinary account of the experience of selflessness."
        —Joseph Goldstein, Author of *The Experience of Insight*

"*Collision with the Infinite* is an amazingly honest, fascinating, and vivid account of one woman's awakening to her essential emptiness. In fact this awakening is available to all who dare to look in at the infinite."

        —Douglas Harding, author of *On Having No Head*

In Quest of God
by Swami Ramdas
ISBN: 1-884997-01-5   190pp $10.95

"One of the most remarkable testimonies in the annals of world mysticism."
—Eknath Easwaran (from the Preface)

"In 1970 I came upon the writings of Swami Ramdas. And there it was, so innocently presented, a testament to the possibility that by remembering Ram (God), one's life could be transformed, totally transformed, moment by moment, into divine 'lila' (play)."
—Ram Dass (Richard Alpert) from the Foreword

Comparable in lasting significance to the famous classics *The Way of a Pilgrim* and Brother Lawrence's *The Practice of the Presence of God*. The narrative contains many inspiring accounts of how his pure love transformed people who at first treated him very harshly. This extraordinary spiritual autobiography recounts the story of a homeless monk's journey.

In the Vision of God - volumes I & II
by Swami Ramdas
ISBN: 1-884997-03-1 & 1-884997-05-8   280pp $14.95 each

These two books conclude the trilogy of Swami Ramdas that started with *In Quest of God*. They continue an account of his pilgrimage across the length and breadth of India as a penniless pilgrim. Witty, yet inspiringly and compellingly told.

The Play of God—
Visions of the Life of Krishna
by Vanamali,
Preface by Eknath Easwaran
ISBN: 1-884997-07-4   416pp $19.95

"This book is going to become a classic text which opens many doors—doors historical, cultural and inspirational."
—*Publishers Weekly*

"Vanamali has provided a useful book that gives the events of Krishna's life and their spiritual message. Vanamali's presentation of the spiritual message behind each story makes the book interesting reading. She uses a chronological approach to Krishna's birth and childhood, followed by stories of his youth, his adulthood, and the 'death' of the one who is deathless. Highly recommended as a fresh and readable presentation, in English, of the life and meaning of Krishna."
—*Library Journal*

Peace Pilgrim's Wisdom

by Peace Pilgrim, edited by Cheryl Canfield
ISBN: 1-884997-11-2   224pp $14

Peace Pilgrim was a genuine American saint who for 28 years lived on the road in faith, not accepting money or asking for food or shelter. She was a witness for inner and outer peace. Cheryl Canfield spent much time with her and helped compile and edit, along with four others, *Peace Pilgrim—Her Life and Work in Her Own Words*, currently with over 400,000 copies in print. This inspirational book has one of her sayings for each day of the year.

Treasury of Spiritual Wisdom

compiled by Andy Zubko
ISBN: 1-884997-10-4   510pp $19.95

A collection of over 10,000 spiritually oriented sayings, from sages, saints and others, providing cutting insights and uncommon wisdom. The entries are divided into 142 categories such as silence, love, peace, relationships and death. Compiled by a devotee of Ramana Maharshi and Peace Pilgrim.
"These pithy bits make good reading."
        —*Publishers Weekly*

"This 'Bartlett's Quotations for the Soul' is a massive collection of inspirational quotations...Because it will be appropriate for use by students, teachers, and seekers, this handy reference will be a strong addition to all collections. Recommended."
        —*Library Journal*

The Nectar of Immortality

by Sri Nisargadatta Maharaj, edited by Robert Powell
ISBN 1-884997-13-9   186pp $14

"The singular pursuit of the awakened person is to find that part of himself or herself that cannot be destroyed by death. I know of no one who can aid you more on that journey than Nisargadatta Maharaj. Let him be with you, as he is always with me, via this profound book, *The Nectar of Immortality*."
        —Wayne Dyer, author of *Your Sacred Self*

Available from fine bookstores or directly from the publisher:
Blue Dove Press
P. O. Box 261611
San Diego, CA 92196
telephone: (619)271-0490